Out of the Darkness

An Expose' of the Metaphysical World

Crystal Snow-Hebel

DEDICATION

This book is affectionately dedicated first and foremost to the Lord, Jesus Christ, our soon coming King. It is written for His glory, and the furthering of His Kingdom. It is then dedicated to all believers. My hope is that by sharing the story of how I was deeply involved in the metaphysical world while thinking I was getting closer to God, it will shed light on some practices that have seeped into believer's lives under the disguise of "Spiritualism". The enemy is still arraying himself as an angel of light, but my hope is to open the eyes of those who may have been spiritually blinded.

CONTENTS

Introduction   Pg.1

1   The Lie   Pg.3

2   Tarot Cards and Psychic Readings   Pg.10

3   Meditation Groups   Pg. 19

4   Qigong & the "Harvesting" of Energy   Pg.28

5   Yoga   Pg.41

6   Energy Workshops   Pg.57

7   Crystal Healings   Pg.68

8   Channeling Spirits & Spirit Guides   Pg.79

9   Divining Rods   Pg.88

10   Reiki Healing   Pg.96

11   Mercy said "No"   Pg.107

12   I Give Unto You Power!   Pg.119

ACKNOWLEDGMENTS

I would like to acknowledge the love and support from my family, friends, and all those who have encouraged me, covered me in prayer, and supported me during the writing of this book.

To Linda Arzu who pre-read my manuscript and provided much insight, wisdom and feedback; thank you from the bottom of my heart. This book wouldn't be what it is today without your help!

Thank you to my daughter, Courtney, for creating my book's cover. The Lord showed us the same vision, and then you brought it to life!

Thank you to Shannon Turner, my Book Writing Consultant. I believe the Lord brought you into my life to help me birth this book. You kept me on track with my weekly deadlines and shared a wealth of knowledge with me; enabling me to bring this from a long-time dream and desire to the reality of a published work.

Introduction

Do you feel like you were created to make a difference in this world? You were. Do you feel that perhaps you are just a little different from everyone else? You are. Do you feel that God has created you to bring healing, peace, and comfort to those around you who are suffering with an illness or bound by a spirit of fear and anxiety? He has. And God is not the only one who knows it! Whether you know it, acknowledge it, or not, there are forces coming against all of us. Desiring to distract or derail us from the perfect plans and path God has for us. This book is about one such path.

In ignorance, I became completely entrenched in the metaphysical world. While what I was experiencing seemed glorious and miraculous, it was actually leading me to a place of devastation and destruction. Sometimes you don't know you are drowning until you hit the bottom of the ocean floor. Innocence did not keep me from entering into situations meant to completely consume me, but God's love, grace and mercy were enough to pull me out.

Out of the darkness came an opportunity to walk in His marvelous light. Out of the darkness came a beautiful testimony for His glory. Out of the darkness was formed this vessel in response to a 15-year cry of "send me"!
An opportunity to shine the light of the Lord onto weapons that are being formed against His church.

And they overcame him by the blood of the Lamb, and by the word of their testimony... (Revelation 12:11)

This is my testimony.

CHAPTER 1
~ The Lie ~

It was a Sunday morning. I remember this particular Sunday like it was yesterday. There were six of us who had gathered for brunch. We sat at a table located in the front of the restaurant as the morning sun streamed in through the window, warming my back. We were all trying to recover from the long night out the evening before. A dear friend of mine at the time, we will call him Aaron, was there. I counted myself lucky to be sitting right next to him for this meal and was eager to pick his brain about a world that was unknown to me. He had psychic abilities.

Many times, I had seen him walk up to complete strangers with a "word". He would simply walk up and say, "I have a message for you." The people on the receiving end were always intrigued and seemingly open to hearing what Aaron had to say. He would tell them of things that they had already experienced, or things that had not yet come to pass. On many occasions, supposedly connecting them with loved ones who had passed away. These messages were always incredibly descriptive and led people to believe that there must certainly be some truth to what he was sharing. He was always loving, compassionate, and seemed to bring a peace or comfort into the lives of those he spoke into. There was an "energy" around him that I admired and seemed to resonate with.

Throughout our meal I was utterly amazed and hanging on to his every word. He proceeded to tell me of things that he should have no way of knowing! Warning me of paths I should not go down, encouraging me in other areas...how did he know I was even considering these things? Explaining how I felt emotionally about things I was currently going through...What? How could he even know that?

Throughout the rest of brunch, he rambled on about things he was picking up, and shared past experiences of people that he had "read." How he helped them make difficult decisions, how he kept them from entering into dangerous situations, how he revealed secrets. I wanted to be able to do that for people, to help people in that way so badly, I could almost taste it! I remember saying to him "I wish I was psychic." So, the following lie (from the very pit of Hell) changed the trajectory of my life for the next 13 years. His response was: "Crystal, you're one of the most psychic people I've ever met!" To say that I was intrigued, would be the understatement of a lifetime! I was snagged! Hook, line & sinker!

I knew that without a shadow of a doubt, I was created to help people. That the burden and compassion I felt for people was instilled into my very being by the God who created me. I had been labeled many things: empathic (the ability to feel or sense others' emotions), a healer, compassionate, or just being "in tune" with those around me but psychic was never one of them. All I did know was that God had put certain things inside of me. I did not know at the time they were supposed to be used for His glory, but the devil sure did!

From this moment on, I would delve into anything (and I do mean anything) that felt like it was meant to fine tune the "gifts" within me. The trouble with that mindset was that I had no real foundation of "truth" beneath me. The enemy of my soul knew this and took every single opportunity to lure me into many, many, many modalities, none of which led down the path that the Lord Himself had prepared before me.

I searched for people who felt like me. People who would understand this burden for humanity. People who could help me understand what I was experiencing and help me to use all of that productively to serve God with the purpose for which He had created me.

I believe, with all my heart, that the Lord allowed me to go through everything that I am about to share with you. He knew that ultimately the desire of my heart was to serve Him. I believe that He walked with me through the "fires of Hell" and kept me with His strong arm of protection. All, so that one day, He could anoint me, His vessel, to sound an alarm for His people. So that I could share firsthand the weapons of warfare being formed against His church! That He would one day, this day, take what the devil meant for evil, and turn it for good to save many lives.

The word of God tells us in Rev 12:11 that the brethren overcame the devil "by the blood of the Lamb, and by the word of their testimony." I have waited 15 long years while saying, crying, even at times screaming at the top of my lungs, "send me," for the Lord to give me the liberty to share this testimony with you. Why the 15-year wait? He needed to refine me into a strong enough vessel to be able to fight and withstand what is assuredly going to come against me as I reveal the conniving ways of the powers and principalities that have chosen to exalt themselves and come against the people and knowledge of God. You would never send a baby amidst a battlefield and expect it to be able to fight and survive, right? Our beautiful Heavenly Father wouldn't either, thank God! The Lord has purged, pruned, and pressed me in His loving kindness, laying precept upon precept, so that I may walk in the power of His Holy Spirit to help bring awareness, His truth, and His light, into the darkest of places.

So, this is my testimony. As I hope you have surmised, all of this begins before I knew God. This is my journey to God. As you travel down these memory lanes with me, it is important that you understand that I thought that everything I was experiencing was a gift from God, and that He, Himself, was using me mightily. I know now that the devil can certainly array himself as an angel of light and has entrapped many poor souls with the same lie and facade. As I start sharing the details of what I saw and lived through, you will see that I was undoubtedly in the midst of a supernatural world, but it was not of God. I could only describe the things that were manifesting before me as miraculous, and all I did know was that it didn't come from me. So, logically, (in my mind) I could only devise it all must have come from God. Jesus, our merciful Savior, winked at my ignorance and saw my heart. It is truly by His grace and mercy alone that I am still here today and am able to share this for His glory, and the furthering of His Kingdom!

It would be an incredibly sad story, and of no effect or Godly purpose if I was only to share the snares of the devil. Oh, but hallelujah! The best part of the story comes when you will see the Lord, God Almighty, step in with His love, grace, mercy, and sheer power of His Holy Spirit to deliver me from the nasty snares of the fowl, unclean spirits that I had unknowingly welcomed into my life, and physical body. But we have much to go through before we get there.

The last thing I want to emphasize before we really delve in is that while I did acknowledge and trust that there was a God, I did not have a relationship with Him. I had never read the Bible; therefore, I had no knowledge of His word. That being said, I did not have it as a foundation to stand on, nor did I know that I could have looked to it for guidance. Worst of all, I did not have any way of knowing that I was being led away, far away, from where I was supposed to be going, into places that I didn't belong and had no business being. And in many instances, that's how the devil gets us! Think about his tactics that go all the way back to what he did with Adam and Eve.

God had prepared a beautiful land; a garden with trees, herbs, flowers, a river that I'm sure, had to be absolutely breathtaking! The Lord had prepared a place of perfection for His people. I'm thinking that every day the weather was picture perfect, maybe 77 degrees, sun shining, zero humidity, and a perfect gentle breeze. The river watered the land, the trees supplied the food to eat. And I'm pretty sure the fruit had to be top notch deeeelicious! There was only one rule...

they were not supposed to eat the fruit that came from the tree of knowledge of good and evil. So, on what do you think the devil got Adam and Eve to focus? Yeah, the tree of knowledge of good and evil. And can't you just hear his conniving, manipulating voice? "… And he said unto the woman, Yea, hath God said, Ye shall not eat of every tree of the garden? (Genesis 3:1) After all, wasn't it a tree that God Himself had placed in the garden amidst the other trees? Didn't it produce fruit just like the other trees? But this one was going to give them knowledge!

All Satan had to do was get them to do something that would seemingly profit them, seemingly be a good idea, and have them believe that it was not really far off from what God had intended. And, guess what? He had them hook, line and sinker! You see, God had intended to bless them! To feed them from every tree…every fruit that they had found desirable, but one! He desired for them to keep their innocence. What an amazing blessing that was, right? Can you imagine still living in that bliss?

So, like it happens with many of us, they stepped off God's perfect path onto a shiny, glittery, smoke-filled path of the devil that was laced with bells and whistles…leading to death, spiritual death.

A similar story, my story, is about to reveal a similar tragedy. The devil knew that God had desired to bless me, to use me (as He does you), all he had to do to get me was to show me something so similar to God's path and plan, entice or lure me to something that made sense to me. That seemingly matched what I thought was God's plan. After all, didn't God intend to use me to heal His people? To bring peace to the storms raging in loved ones' lives? To bring deliverance to those bound and held captive? Peace and comfort to the heavy laden? Even freedom from demonic possession? Of course, He did! Those are all the things for which He desires to use every person in His body, His church!

That is why He gave us the keys to the Kingdom!
Matthew16:19 states

...I will give unto thee the keys of the kingdom of heaven; and whatsoever thou shalt bind on earth shall be bound in heaven; and whatsoever thou shalt loose on earth shall be loosed in heaven.

Jesus promised comfort and wisdom:

But the Comforter, which is the Holy Ghost, whom the Father will send in my name, he shall teach you all things, and bring all things to your remembrance, whatsoever I have said unto you. (John 14:26)

Jesus promised power over the enemy of our souls:

...ye shall receive power, after that the Holy Ghost is come upon you (Acts 1:8)
Behold, I give unto you power to tread on serpents and scorpions, and over all the power of the enemy; and nothing shall by any means hurt you. (Luke 10:19)

Jesus Himself told us that similar signs to the ones I desired after should in fact follow His people:

And these signs shall follow them that believe; In my name shall they cast out devils; they shall speak with new tongues; They shall take up serpents; and if they drink any deadly thing, it shall not hurt them; they shall lay hands on the sick, and they shall recover.
(Mark 16: 17-18)

Notice in the scripture above it says, **"In my name."** So, what the devil showed and promised me was that I was going to see and experience signs similar to those listed above (because the devil surely does have some power), but **none** of them were going to be in the name of Jesus Christ! And **none** of that was placing me on a path that led to His salvation or to the Lord's Heavenly Kingdom. Where was it leading? To where the Bible describes as a place of everlasting fire that was originally prepared for the devil and his angels. (Matthew 25:41) A place of weeping (Matthew 8:12), wailing and gnashing of teeth (Matthew 13:42), darkness (Matthew 25:30), torments (Luke 16:23) and everlasting punishment (Revelation 20:10).

When the Lord's truth is revealed, and the smoke is cleared from the devil's paths, we can see that it always leads to destruction, devastation, and spiritual death. That, in a nutshell, is what happened to me. The next several chapters are going to describe what I experienced while completely blinded and walking in darkness. Though, in my sight, it looked beautiful, even miraculous, until the Lord Himself took the veil off my clouded eyes. He showed me who I was serving and the sheer ugliness of the world in which I had become entrenched…the world leading, pulling, and drawing me to death. But again, Hallelujah for Jesus Christ and His resurrecting power!

CHAPTER 2
Tarot Cards and Psychic Readings

~ What the enemy wanted me to think ~

Back to the beginning of my journey to the darkest of places.
Over the next several months, I would spend hours upon hours
with Aaron while he "trained" me to be psychic. Initially, we
would hold hands, as he would concentrate on a specific
emotion. He instructed me to be "open" and "receive" what
he was sending. He would send that "energy" through my
hands, and I would try to tell him what he was feeling. The
more time we spent on this exercise of "sharing feelings," the
easier it got. I started being able to sense his emotions, as well
as send mine back to him, always astonished and pleasantly
pleased when we were reiterating back to each other what was
being sent. This was just the beginning of what I thought was
the most amazing gift I had ever received.

Before long, he instructed me to buy my first deck of Tarot
cards. Excited to embark on this new branch of my journey,
I headed out to a local new-age store. As I walked into the
shop, it was as if there was a presence welcoming me, greeting
me. As if something, someone, had been waiting for me with
open, beckoning arms. (The devil is always celebrating, and
eager to help someone onto a path that leads to devastation
and death. So, you bet! Welcoming arms!)

There was a feel of magic to the place. There was soothing
music playing; flutes and chimes if I recall correctly. The
atmosphere was filled with smoke and the fragrance of
incense. The sunbeams streaking in through stained-glass
windows, cutting through the haze of the incense added to the

ambiance and a feeling of being embraced and escorted into a world that was special and for a chosen few.

Upon asking for direction, I was instructed that the Tarot card section was in the back left of the store with an approving nod & smile of the shop owner. (As I look back through spiritual eyes, I can see the glare of the demon that must have been thinking "We've got another one!") My expectation and excitement mounted as I walked on the worn Chinese rug to the back of the store. There were shelves upon mystical shelves of them. I remember picking up several decks of cards, one by one, and waiting for some kind of sign that one deck was the deck chosen for me. That that specific deck would connect me to the psychic world and reveal unspoken secrets of the universe to me. That would be the deck used by the angelic realm, to give messages to people from heavenly places. That would be the deck used by those who had passed away or crossed over (as they say in the metaphysical world), to relay messages to loved ones still "on this side." There was a lot of weight on choosing the right deck. It had to be perfect! I had to "feel" its energy and know without a shadow of a doubt that I was choosing the exact one meant for me.

After what may have been hours, I was sure I had found the right one. The pictures were somewhat whimsical, with soft, muted pastel colors. I bought a workbook on reading cards that came with explicit and easy to follow instructions and exercises. This also had to be the perfect tool and took me quite some time to pick out as well. Another book I purchased was someone's account on their readings and psychic experiences. I was excited to read someone's psychic encounters and thought I could use this as encouragement and something that I would aspire to attain.

While in the store, I rummaged through a variety of incense sticks and found some that were supposed to invoke the spirit realm, and some that were supposed to be helpful in angelic readings. Of course, I got those, along with some that were supposed to induce a meditative state, and some others that just plain smelled pretty. I left the shop that day feeling equipped with the tools necessary to direct this new course of my life.

My study sessions with Aaron were intense and emotional. He explained it was because I was an "emotional reader"; meaning I easily connected with the emotions of whomever I was reading for. Through meditation and practice, I would also learn how to connect with the "energies" of the cards. Now, instead of holding hands, Aaron would think of and feel an emotion, but I was supposed to use the tarot deck to discern what it was. He showed me how to fan out the cards in my left hand, face down. I would close my eyes and try to be "open" to the cards. I would run my right hand under the cards (on the face side) back and forth until I could "feel" the card I was supposed to choose. I was surprised how easily I could connect with, and more times than not pull a card that directly related to what Aaron was thinking about or feeling. Each card had a simple explanation or meaning to it.

In the beginning, I had typed up the potential meaning of each card and tacked it to the wall in front of my desk. As I was "led" to pull a card, I would quickly look up at my list, and start to read what I had typed pertaining to that card. Then somehow, this "psychic ability" would take over and embellish on it. Eventually, I memorized the specific meaning of each card, and found it easier and easier to allow what just seemed like a download of information to flow through me in the form of what I believed were messages from "the other side." The more time I spent doing readings, the easier it was to pick up specific details that related to someone's scenario. I remember vividly seeing people. A description I would give would sound something like this: "I see a gentleman. He has a roundish face. There is a dark spot on the left side of his face… maybe a mole? He is balding on the top of his head but has hair around his ears. He has a solid build, a little on the heavy side." The person I was reading might say "Oh! That's Harry!" I would continue: "He is sitting in a worn, brown armchair." "That was his favorite chair! He always sat in that chair!" and the reading went on, me just describing what I saw, or repeating what I heard. There seemed to be something extremely magical happening with this deck of cards.

I remember purchasing other psychic decks. One was called angel cards and was supposed to give specific answers to questions asked from the angelic realm. I also remember having a second tarot deck, but I usually resorted back to using the initial one I purchased. The more worn it became, the easier it was to use to read.

One morning, there was a specific instance I vividly remember as I did an exercise with the cards that I got out of the workbook I had purchased. It asked me to pick a card from my deck. In the card I chose, there was a woman leaning over a stream. The woman, actually the whole card, was quite beautiful and portrayed a serene landscape in the background. The book instructed me to hold the card and close my eyes. To clear my mind and open myself up to what was going to be given. Now, I know this is going to sound absurd, but I am not going to hold anything back for fear of being judged, nor will I sugar coat things that I experienced. I felt like I had "entered" the card. I leaned over the stream and could feel the coolness and hear the sound of the running water. I could smell a sweet fragrance emanating from the forest that was depicted on the card. It was beautiful! I could feel a soft, warm breeze on my face, and I felt a sense of peace and healing wash over me. A place of magic! And I felt that in a moment, I had been completely connected to the psychic world. I had been given a gift of "awakening" to a spiritual realm. In my excitement, I tried to explain my experience to my boyfriend, (now my husband of 28 years), he was, and rightfully so, nervous about me somehow getting "stuck" there. And, boy, did I! Spiritually speaking.

I thus began opening a door to the demonic realm, that I was in no way prepared to deal with and had no way of closing. The more I practiced, the more I could see, feel, and receive from the spirit realm. I literally could not get enough! I would spend my lunch hours in the car, listening to mystical music and reading the book I bought about the writer's psychic memoirs. After each scenario, the desire to help people the way I thought that writer was, became increasingly overwhelming…almost desperate.

I offered readings to everyone I knew, eager for practice, and getting "fine-tuned" for receiving and giving messages to loved ones. I gotta say here, that it is utterly amazing how easily people will follow you down paths that lead to destruction, but oh my goodness! The battle is real when you try to lead them down a path that leads to true salvation.

Aaron told me that I should get a name for my "business"; I chose Crystal Visions. He said I should make up business cards, pamphlets, obtain a tax ID number, and register my business. I promptly did all those things.

At that time, Aaron was a reader for a well-known Network that provided psychic readings for people who called in. That was a real big deal, back in the day. One day he says to me "Ok Crystal, you're ready! Time to apply for a position on the Network!" I remember thinking "really"? I mean, at the time, there were commercials on TV for that Network and everything! Famous people were calling in for readings! Could I pull that off? Was I really ready? I was certainly going to try!

One morning, after spending some meditation moments with my deck of cards, I called the number Aaron had given me to ask for an interview from the network. From what Aaron had explained, this basically entailed doing a reading for someone enabling them to verify if there was really any psychic ability, and how accurate the reading would be. I wanted this so badly. I remember being so nervous that my hands were sweaty and shaky as I dialed the phone. I was thinking this here was a make-or-break situation. This supposed gift would be validated, and I would continue to grow, move, and operate in the spirit realm...or be forced to move onto something else. I had recently had a baby. I had been laid off from work after eight years, in the eighth month of pregnancy due to a company downsizing, and we certainly needed the income! When someone answered after what seemed to be an endless time of ringing on the other end, my voice started quivering as I asked to speak to someone in reference to becoming one of their readers. I was taken aback and caught a little off guard when the voice on the other side of the phone answered promptly "Ok, go ahead...read me." What? Right now? Just like that? I told the guy that I really needed this job, that I was incredibly nervous, and I did not want to blow an opportunity to work for them.

Now, the following response from him should have let me know that this company did not truly have the best interest of their callers at heart. (Big shock, right? A company run by the enemy of our souls not having an interest in the well-being of its callers?) Apparently, there really was no bar or level of expectancy that had to be met before getting hired, because what he told me was "Ok, let's get your nerves out of the way, you're hired." He told me to grab a pen and write down the ID number that was assigned to me. This is a number of which the callers would be informed. In the event they received a good reading, they could call and ask to be reconnected specifically with you by that ID number for a future reading; thus, allowing you to build your own clientele base. We were to be paid a certain dollar amount for every minute of the call. (I do not recall what that dollar amount was currently.) I confirmed what I thought I had heard. "You mean, I got the job?" He told me that I did, and then gently asked that I go ahead and give him a reading with my tarot cards. I did. And so, began my psychic reading business. I worked for that network for quite some time, often receiving repeat calls from individuals who were eager to reconnect with me and the spirits that were using me to deliver messages from a realm that is beyond ours.

From there, with great excitement, I started handing out my business cards to the masses! Eager to help the people who needed help. To bring comfort to the people who were heartbroken and longing to be reconnected to love ones who had passed away. To give direction to those who were feeling lost. After all, I am thinking, this is what God created me for. I started booking psychic parties, where friends and loved ones would fill their homes with guests, who would one-by-one come into a room that I had filled with draperies of blue and purple, moons and stars. The atmosphere was always prepared and set with an ambiance of mystical music, incense, and candles. If people who were in attendance booked a party with their own guests, I would "bless" them with a free reading. I would also sign up for spots in local flea markets. I set up a tent filled with all those things listed above, as well as an angel fountain with running water and plants for extra Feng Shui benefits. (One belief of Feng Shui is that the placement of specific objects in very specific locations increases the energy flow of the atmosphere.)   At one particular occasion, the line to my tent was so long, people were waiting about an hour just to talk with me! Actually, standing in line to pay for my psychic services! Hence, I was able to contribute income to our household as my business started flourishing.

~What God wants you to know ~

While the intent of my heart was to help people, I was doing things contrary to the word of God, and the actual plan and purpose for which He had created me!

First, if God Himself gives you a gift, heaven forbid you charge people for sharing it!

Freely you have received, freely give. (Matthew 10:8)

Furthermore, I later learned that these messages were coming from familiar spirits. The Bible describes the scenario when Lucifer (the devil) was kicked out of Heaven. It says ⅓ of the angelic hosts who followed him were also kicked out. (Revelation 12:4) I believe that those are the demonic entities that roam this earth, along with Satan to see whom they can devour. Those were the entities or spirits I was connecting to during these readings. Those spirits are familiar! Familiar with the people coming for the readings. It was that demonic realm that would relay messages to me from what they had been witnessing or observing about the unsuspecting individual who was just trying to receive help, direction or comfort. The word of God is extremely clear and explicit concerning calling upon these spirits for guidance.

We should not call on anyone but Jesus Christ, the Almighty God!

Thou shalt have no other gods before me:
(Exodus 20:3)

Anything or anyone we call upon and trust to give us guidance with the wisdom, knowledge and understanding attributed to God alone, is essentially taking God's place in our sight, minds, and hearts.

For thou shalt worship no other god; for the LORD, whose name is Jealous, is a jealous God (Exodus 34:14)

He is a jealous God! Isn't that amazing? He is jealous over us! He alone wants to be our provider, protector, and way maker. And, in reality, He alone is truly capable!

We should not entertain, give attention, or consideration to familiar spirits:

17

Regard not them that have familiar spirits, neither seek after wizards, to be defiled by them: I am the LORD your God. (Leviticus 19:31)

And when they shall say unto you, seek unto them that have familiar spirits, and unto wizards that peep, and that mutter: should not a people seek unto their God? For the living to the dead? (Isaiah 8:19)

And the soul that turneth after such as have familiar spirits, and after wizards, to go a whoring after them, I will even set my face against that soul, and will cut him off from among his people. (Leviticus 20:6)

Unknowingly, I was allowing myself to be used by Satan's army! Not only is God's word so clear pertaining to staying away from anything related to this whole scenario I was becoming so heavily involved with, but there came a moment when He, in His infinite mercy winked at my ignorance, and opened my eyes to whom I was actually serving. I will share that blood curdling, bone chilling moment at the end of all the other paths and modalities into which the devil had lured me.

CHAPTER 3
Meditation Groups

~ What the enemy wanted me to think ~

For the next 13 years, I was consumed with every aspect of the metaphysical world. I had an insatiable appetite for what I *thought* God was calling me to. So, in search of people who were like-minded, people who were on a quest to develop what I was still certain were God-given abilities, I attended any metaphysical gathering I heard about. I met a sea of people all in search of something. You know, I've gotta say this. Lest those of us who are born again or know the word of God wrongfully judge. Every, and I mean EVERY person I met while delving into this world was either hurt (physically, emotionally, or spiritually) or looking for healing with no true knowledge that it can only be found in God alone. Or, they had a huge, compassionate heart, looking for ways to bring healing to a hurting world; again, not knowing that true healing can only come from the Lord, Jesus Christ.

The first group of people I found met weekly in an old Victorian looking house painted with a variety of blues, purples & yellows. Everything in this new world always seemed so colorful! (This reminds me of something I read on Facebook one day…it read something like this: If the grass looks greener on the other side of the fence, it could be located over a septic tank. Yeah, pretty accurate here!) Anyway, I believe this was my first introduction to the "white light."
Starting in this small group, and in almost all modalities I had gotten involved with, I was taught to surround myself with a

white light. It was explained that this was necessary to protect ourselves from any evil that wanted to penetrate our atmosphere, and impact what we had intended for good with an alternative plan. This light was supposed to be "good, pure, clean, and protective" energy. We were instructed to call upon powers that be, gods, goddesses, energies of the universe, angelic hosts, mother nature, spirit guides, pretty much any entities that were waiting and wanting to help us from the spirit realm...anything but Jesus, Himself.

I had never endeavored or embarked on something completely new when it involved a group of people I had never met before all by myself. This was a first for me, and I remember being so proud of myself for mustering up the courage to do it as I walked up the stone steps and knocked on the door. In that small Victorian house, we sat in a room that had been cleared of furniture except for a circle of chairs arranged on an apparently heavily trafficked and worn hardwood floor. Huge windows gave way to an amazing amount of sunlight that filled the room. After we had all invoked this "white light of protection," we were instructed to hold hands, clear our minds, and open ourselves and channels for a spiritual connection. The gentleman hosting the event told us that he was going to start sending "an energy" around the circle. We should be open, allow that energy to flow in through one hand, through our bodies, and out through the other hand, thus allowing "it" to gain power and impact as "it" traveled around the circle.

Thinking back, I recall thinking that maybe I felt something, but was a little jealous that others had apparently experienced something far greater than I did. They were saying things like "Wow! Did you feel that? That was amazing!" Not wanting to let on that I myself did not have a major breakthrough with this "energy thing," just smiled, nodded, and quietly agreed. Honestly, this just ignited a greater desire to really tap into this mystical world. So, I kept searching.

I attended drumming circles, seances, other meditation groups, and any gathering where I thought I could be fed into and increase my ability to connect with the spirit realm. One day, I was led to a group that I would soon consider to be my spiritual family, and a place where the devil and/or soldiers of his army would use to drag me to the depths of darkness. This group was led by a woman we will call Tracey.

Trying to remember now, but I think we met weekly, on a Wednesday evening for a minimal fee. In my eyes, Tracey was amazing! She had many psychic gifts and abilities. These meditation groups were powerful, insightful, and filled with love! Tracey was the "host" to many spirits. These spirits assigned a name to themselves and spoke as one entity through her. Many spirits, speaking through one voice, simultaneously. In these meditation groups, we would fill her living room. Every chair, couch, and spot on the floor was taken, as we eagerly called upon the powers that be for protection, cleared our minds, and waited upon those spirits to share their message and wisdom from the other side. Out of this group, a core group developed, and became remarkably close. Over the next several years, we would share many experiences together as we trained, and embarked on new depths of the supernatural world. It was with this group that I delved into channeling spirits myself, crystal healings, reiki healings and more...but we'll get there.

In the initial meditation meetings, Tracey would explain that she would step aside (inside of herself) and allow the spirits to use her body to communicate with us. She would ask us to please stay seated once the session began, because if someone were to get up and leave the room in the midst of it, it would cause a "tear" in the atmosphere and be uncomfortable for her. You could actually feel the atmosphere shift or change like there was a new thickness or substance to it when these spirits showed up! The kind of change that gives you goosebumps or causes the hairs on your arms and back of your neck to stand up. They would come with an extremely specific message for the group, but after they were done speaking, the floor was open for questions. You could literally ask about *anything* and they would seemingly have an answer... and it was always seemingly a good one! If you were interested, you could book an individual session with Tracey, where those spirits would come bearing messages for you directly. You could take those "spiritual conversations" in any direction you wanted. I, of course, booked a few of those sessions for myself over the years.

Because of the interest generated in that meditation group, Tracey started workshops...all kinds of workshops! Some newer individuals would even show up to our meditation group, and "enlighten" us with new modalities. They, too, would offer training sessions in these spiritual realms of wonderment. We, this core group of seekers, linked arms, and walked through them together. We were all so grateful for each other, the love we all had for each other, for humanity, and the fact that we all would sacrifice so much of our time and effort to become better vessels for the gifts that were being imparted to us. We were comfortable enough with each other to allow ourselves to be vulnerable as we tested new waters and methods. All in the name of being better servants to humanity.

~ What God wants you to know ~

About Meditation:

Meditation is described as a way of directing or redirecting your thoughts. It is a practice of focusing on something specific or in many instances, focusing on nothing at all. A practice of clearing your mind completely, allowing you to achieve higher states of awareness or consciousness.

The word of God tells us that we need to protect our minds, hearts and souls! We cannot be open to, or subject ourselves to, whatever doctrine the wind (or devil) carries our way! If we open our minds, ourselves, to "whatever" is out there, and "whatever" wants to come in, trust me! You are extending an invitation to so much more than you realize! Your invitation will be accepted, but you certainly will not be led to any place good.

The Bible gives very explicit instructions for exactly what we should meditate on:

*This book of the law shall not depart out of thy mouth; but thou shalt **meditate** therein day and night, that thou mayest observe to do according to all that is written therein: for then thou shalt make thy way prosperous, and then thou shalt have good success. (Joshua 1:8)*

Again, it is only the knowledge of the word of God that keeps a sound and secure foundation underneath you. The foundation that leads to salvation and everlasting joy!

*I will **meditate** in thy precepts (teachings) and have respect unto thy ways. I will delight myself in thy statutes: I will not forget thy word. (Psalm 119: 15-16)*

Finally, brethren, whatsoever things are true, whatsoever things are honest, whatsoever things are just, whatsoever things are pure, whatsoever things are lovely, whatsoever things are of good report; if there be any virtue, and if there be any praise, think on these things. (Philippians 4:8)

The Bible is given to us for guidance...in everything! To lead and redirect us when we are heading in a destructive direction. That we may be perfect! God only wants good things for us!

All scripture is given by inspiration of God, and is profitable for doctrine, for reproof, for correction, for instruction in righteousness: That the man of God may be perfect, thoroughly

furnished unto all good works.
(2 Timothy 3:16-17)

White light of protection:

Had I known the word of God; I would have known that there is no such thing as a white light of protection! That just because something appears to be ok, or of God, does not mean that it truly is.

...Satan himself is transformed into an angel of light (2 Corinthians 11:14)

There is a seemingly beautiful side of evil...but it is certainly **NOT** beautiful! In truth, I was actually surrounding myself with nothing but the demonic realm. Of course, it was pretty! Of course, it felt calming and peaceful! The devil is certainly not going to gain any souls by showing his true colors! Nor will he allow you to discover his true essence while you are serving him. If he did, you would not continue! And you would want him out of your life! The deal is, if you invite him in, you have surrendered the power and authority that the Lord came to give you over him. And he will not leave just because you ask him to. You can believe me on this point also! He is going to put up quite a fight for you, and it will take someone (or several people in my case) operating in the power of the Holy Spirit to set you free! But know this with assurance! There IS FREEDOM, in Jesus Christ!

If the word of God says to stay clear of something...stay clear! If someone tells you something is of God, but it is not in His word...run! And if you are dealing with something spiritual? The Bible says this:

BELOVED, believe not every spirit, but try the spirits whether they are of God: because many false prophets are gone out into the world. Hereby know ye the Spirit of God:

*Every spirit that confesseth that Jesus Christ is come in the
flesh is of God: And every spirit that confesseth not that
Jesus Christ is come in the flesh is not of God: and this is
that spirit of antichrist, whereof ye have heard that it should
come; and even now already is it in the world.*
(1 John 4:1-3)

A person can be possessed by many devils at one time, and
they can speak as one voice. In the Bible, there was such a
man who was dwelling amidst the tombs. The demons within
that man were so strong that he could not be held nor bound
by chains for he would just break them. The demons
tormented that man day and night...driving him to cut himself
with stones. (Once the devil is revealed, he will always cause
great torment as he did with me...keep reading!) When Jesus
approached that man, he asked the spirit "...*What is thy name?
And he answered, saying, my name is Legion: for we are
many.*" *(Mark 5:9)* See that? Many demons, speaking as one.

So...yeah, the metaphysical world operates in the name of
many things...but none of them is the name of Jesus! They
do not attribute the Godhead and all His glorious powers,
wisdom, knowledge and understanding that belong to the
Lord alone, to Jesus. The devil is *still* trying to steal His glory!

My Goodness! You would think he'd learn! He never did,
never can, and never will! It was the very reason he got kicked
out of Heaven in the first place. He was all lifted up in pride.

See for yourself in God's word:

*How art thou fallen from heaven, O Lucifer, son of the
morning! How art thou cut down to the ground, which didst
weaken the nations! For thou has said in thine heart, **I will**
ascend into heaven, **I will** exalt my throne above the stars of
God; **I will** sit also upon the mount of the congregation, in
the sides of the north: **I will** ascend above the heights of the
clouds, **I will** be like the most High. (Isaiah 14:12-14)*

Side note: all these self-help courses and classes that are now available...The ones that teach **I am** able, **I will** do, **I will** accomplish, **I will** overcome are not necessarily positive influences or Godly instructions. Anything that teaches you that *you* are the one completely in control, that all power and ability lies within *yourself* and that all things are possible if *you* just put your mind to it, does not line up with God's word. Jesus is the only one completely in control. And all things are possible...with God!

I can do all things through Christ which strengtheneth me.
(Philippians 4:13)

With God all things are possible. (Matthew 19:26)

We need to be careful not to lift ourselves up in pride and remember that all we do should be for the glory of God.

For by him were all things were created, that are in heaven,
and that are in earth, visible and invisible, whether they be
thrones, or dominions, or principalities, or powers: all
*things were created by him and **for him.** (Colossians 1:16)*

The enemy of our soul often lures people to serve him by offering power and an opportunity to exalt ourselves. In a nutshell, anything that you are considering being involved with, anything that promises self-development that does not ultimately point to, direct others to, or bring Glory to God but to self, should be kept in check. Of course, the Lord wants us to succeed, to be profitable, responsible, dependable, etc. But honestly, He never wants us to take our eyes off Him and think we can do things separate from Him. He should *always* be our ultimate focus! The Bible warns us against putting all our faith and focus on ourselves. We must recognize that we accomplish things, because He has given us the ability to do so. He will align people in our lives, to provide whatsoever

26

we need. He wants us to succeed but warns us against boasting in ourselves. All glory goes to Jesus!

Go to now, ye that say, Today or tomorrow we will go into such a city, and continue there a year, and buy and sell, and get gain: Whereas ye know not what shall be on the morrow. For what is your life? It is even a vapour, that appeareth for a little time, and then vanisheth away. For that ye out to say, If the Lord will, we shall live, and do this or that. ***But now ye rejoice in your boasting: all such rejoicing is evil.*** *Therefore, to him that knoweth to do good, and doeth it not, to him it is sin. (James 4:13-17)*

And whatsoever ye do, do it heartily, as to the Lord, and not unto men; Knowing that of the Lord ye shall receive the reward of the inheritance: for ye serve the Lord Christ. (Colossians 3:23-24)

Bottom line here is it is okay to want to do and be better. If you look unto the Lord, allow Him to establish your thoughts and order your steps, you will be!

CHAPTER 4
Qigong & the "Harvesting" of Energy

~ What the enemy wanted me to think ~

So, you know how I had stated that Tracey held many workshops for this group of people that gathered weekly in her house? One of the sessions she orchestrated for us was a weekend-long training in Qigong. (Pronounced Chee-Gong) We will call the guy who led that training Ted.

He opened the session on an early Friday morning with an amazing slideshow of expeditions and travels he had been on. Sometimes obviously putting himself into dangerous positions, seemingly jeopardizing his own safety, all to capture the "perfect shot." These were places of which you would dream. Places all over the world. From the top of the highest mountains, to fields filled with flowers, to breathtaking ocean views. Truly, the adventures of a lifetime. He said he had done all of that for us! So that we could all soak up the energy or Qi from his experiences. He captured it so that he may share it with us. Wow…we were all certainly impressed and appreciative of what he had done "for us."

There was such a presence, an heir of wisdom, a peace about this guy. Kind of like what you would expect of someone that you would have to climb Mount Everest to see or accomplish some death-defying feat just to get to him. You know, someone not easily attainable. It was like being in the company of a high-up guru, counselor, mentor, master, or sensei type of person filled with the wisdom of the universe. And here he was, with us. Wanting to share all that he had learned, with us. (For a "minimal" fee, of course!)

He introduced us to what Qigong was. He explained that it was an ancient Chinese exercise. We were going to use slow, controlled movements, involving meditation, breathing & healing techniques to achieve higher, healthier versions of ourselves. We were going to connect our minds with the energy sources within our bodies. Somehow, this was supposed to repair the blockages within the energy flow that might have led to sickness, illness and disease. He gave us handouts, and I am sure he also had all kinds of eloquent explanations, but I think that was the gist of it. It was a long time ago, and I haven't thought about the specifics of Qigong in quite a long time.

Before beginning the instructions, he shared with us how he came to know Qigong. How he had traveled to China, the place of its origin, to learn it from some extraordinarily established Masters. Here's the pieces of his story that I recall. He had been excessively sick for a long period of time. The kind of sickness that he suffered from surpassed what the doctors could understand or help with. It was a grievous sickness.

I think I remember him telling us that he was not wealthy nor well off by any means, neither was his family. His family essentially had to make a huge sacrifice to send him to China in hopes that the medicinal techniques found there would bring the healing to what seemed to be a hopeless situation. Ted described the facility in which he stayed. This large stone structure was void of anything resembling "our kind of comfort." No big comfy couches or chairs…no fluffy pillows…certainly not a "resort-kind-of-place." This cold, stony structure (again, from what I do remember) had small bedrooms available for its guests equipped with a small metal-framed bed and thin mattress. Maybe a table? But certainly, no frills.

People came from all over the world, some spending their last dime to get there, to be in the presence of the "Masters" under which they would study. Ted explained that it was so cold and damp that the chill permeated even his bones, adding to the discomfort in which he was already. It was hard to muster enough warmth under the thin blanket supplied to allow his body to relax enough to fall asleep at night. Everyone was freezing! (I guess that was part of the experience or learning process???) He said that regardless of the numerous requests for heat, the people in charge didn't turn it on until they had found someone dead, frozen to death one morning. I know, wow!

Ted explained that his pain by that time was excruciating! Almost unbearable! I asked "How did you find the strength to get out of bed into the freezing morning air? How, in all that pain, did you find the strength to get yourself out into the courtyard where the training would be held each day? And how, once you got out there did you even manage to partake in the physical activities that were being taught?"

I was earnestly asking these questions, because at that time, I felt I could identify with him. You see, I had just been recently diagnosed with Hepatitis C (stupid belly button piercing!) and was undergoing weekly shots of interferon (a type of chemotherapy). This medication had me feeling like I had literally been run over by a truck. I suffered with the whole nine yards of chronic flu-like symptoms. The muscle aches and pains, nausea, and the worst migraines I had ever experienced. There were times I was afraid to roll over in bed for fear of my head splitting right open if I so much as moved a muscle! My "spiritual family" urged me to come to this training as I also might be healed. It was on the expensive side (for my budget) to attend, but I too had become desperate. As I sat there listening to Ted, trying to suppress the pounding in my head enough so I could fully hear what he was saying, and trying desperately not to throw up on the row of people who were unfortunate enough to be sitting right in front of me, all I could think about is how much pain I was in. I wanted to be home, in bed, but I felt like I couldn't even stand up from my chair to get there...let alone start to partake in the exercises that were forthcoming.

Ted's response was that he just kept thinking about the people, the "Masters," who were waiting on him in the courtyard every morning. That they had said they believed in him. That he was there for a specific purpose, and that what he was about to receive (like a "chosen one") would be shared with many. Those dear to me, sitting around me, knew why I had asked. This group looked lovingly, encouragingly to me, as if to say, "We're here for you Crystal, and you can do this!" I decided to trudge forward.

Ted proceeded to explain the "wonders" of this Qigong thing to us. He explained how that by the practice of it he had himself become well...whole again. Certainly, the man standing in front of me seemed to be in perfect shape! Perfect health! If it worked for him, I am thinking I'm going to give this thing my all, and it'll work for me too! As I usually tend to do with things I believe in, I dive in, lock, stock and barrel! 150% all in!

Ted asked us to each find a position facing a blank wall in the room. Swallowing hard, praying for strength, and that I wouldn't throw up, I walked to the back of the room and stood facing the wall. I remember thinking that at least no one could see the wincing in my facial expression, and how appreciative I was for the coolness of the wall against my forehead as I just planted my face into it for support. We were instructed to position our feet straight ahead, facing the wall. Our toes needed to be touching, or close to touching, the wall. We were told to slowly bend at the knees, focusing on not moving our feet or losing our balance until we were in a squatting position. One by one, people fell over, unable to do it...except for two of us. Yes, I did it. It took quite a while, but I did it!

Ted made the two of us feel like "the chosen ones" in this setting. Apparently, that doesn't happen easily for most. Not that it was by any means easy. He asked the two of us to go up on the stage located in the front of the room so that we may "demonstrate" that for everyone. "What?!? Don't make me go up there! I can't even see through my pain right now! Especially after exuding all that effort and energy on the exercise I just did. Surely, I'm gonna puke in front of all of these people! And it's gonna be on stage!!!" Ted urged me. I forget what he said specifically. Something about being part of the process, being richly blessed, blah, blah, blah...I went up. I did it again.

After this portion of the training session, we had a break. Most people flowed out the front door. (Oh, my goodness! I am just remembering now that this was being held in an old, beautiful church! I have not thought of these scenarios in several years but am thankful the Lord is bringing back these memories so vividly enabling me to share them with you!) Walking out the front door, down the steppingstones of the front path, and around the back of that church was a most breath-taking view. I think we were on a mountain top. There were picnic tables, a gazebo, and little gathering areas. Most of us were grouped off into little huddles, giddily sharing the experiences of the morning. I wandered off by myself to find a bench in the shade, wanting to protect my pounding head from the beating sun. I laid down on a bench and called my husband in tears. The pain in my head was intolerable! I remember saying "I can't do this! I am laying down on a bench right now, outside. It hurts so bad! I think I am going to be sick. I don't think I can even make it back inside. How am I going to get home? I don't think I can drive right now." Chris has always been so supportive, in whatever endeavor I embarked. Whether he understood it or not. He asked if I wanted him to come get me. I did want to go home, so badly, but I didn't want to miss out on an opportunity to be healed. What if this was my one chance, the one opportunity orchestrated by God Himself, and I left before receiving His blessing? After listening to Chris' soothing voice of encouragement for a few moments, I decided to tough it out, and stay for the blessing that was promised.

After resting for a time, I made my way back inside for the

next session. As it started, I remember a woman who had been seated a couple chairs away from me had a tickle in her throat. The room was completely silent (as we were instructed to be) except for her continuously clearing her throat as she tried to suppress the cough that apparently needed to happen. One of my dearest loved ones from our core group (we will call her Amy), turned and gave her a mint. Later, Amy shared with me that her spirit guide (This was a spirit that stayed with her, talked with her, instructed her) kept saying "Give her a mint! Give her a mint! Give her a mint!" Amy, as usual, not wanting to be bossed around by this spirit ignored it as long as possible, until it was almost screaming at her: "**Give her a mint**!". She said that she had been so annoyed at the insistence of it. And that certainly gave me a little insight to the gesture of her almost throwing the mint at that poor lady! (I originally thought she was annoyed at the interruption of silence.) I had often found myself jealous over the relationship between Amy and that spirit. They often had full on conversations! Amy didn't necessarily enjoy it. The spirit was overbearing and frequently frightened her. I still found myself coveting the very thing she hated. I will be discussing more on spirits/spirit guides in a later chapter.

A vague recollection of this session prompts me to say that I do remember feeling better at the end of it, somewhat blessed...even chosen. I remember getting home that evening, and Chris was pleasantly surprised at how the pain had obviously decreased within my body. My cats also seemed to notice that something was different. I remember commenting to Chris: "Look at the cats, even they can feel the Qi." Looking back, I'm amazed that they did sense something; however, I'm sure if they had voices, they would have shared with me that it was positively NOT a good thing.

I went back the next morning for the next session eager to delve into this newfound energy. Eager to learn more. The rest of my experiences are a little fuzzy, but I do remember being taught this: the experiences we have create an "energy," good or bad. The positive energies that we create are supposed to be harvested. It is as if, through meditation, you physically gather up the Qi, or energy, and take it into your physical body. The exercises used to harvest these energies are seemingly innocent. Slow, meditative, balanced movements that must be practiced in order to master or perform. These exercises became part of my daily routine, and I did become quite good at them.

One other thing I remember Ted teaching us was that the make-up of the universe was different from what we had been taught or perceived it to be. That what we all experienced while on this earth was part of an intricate grid. That with a trained eye, you could see it, manipulate the energy of it, and operate through it. I think this was a few years before the movie The Matrix came out. Have you seen that one? That movie depicted something like what I had been taught, and "experienced" in the room of that big old beautiful church. All I had to do was concentrate, and change my focus, and I could easily see and "tap into" this grid. It was miraculous! It was amazing! And I certainly felt chosen, or especially gifted, because again not everyone in the room could do this or see this.

It looked like the entire atmosphere was filled with vertical and horizontal lines that moved and flowed around and through every object in existence. The further away objects were, the tighter together the lines were. It looked like it went on infinitely. It is hard to describe, but what I was seeing was spectacular, and it just made sense to my mind's eye. I was thinking: "of course all of existence is part of a grid!" The grid moved with the objects that were within it; all objects, people, and things moved simultaneously, but all within the grid itself. I could instantly see it once it was introduced to me as if a veil had been removed from my eyes in one moment, while others struggled, squinting their eyes and tried ridiculously hard to see what came so easily to me. Why did it come so easily? Why could I see what others couldn't see?

Because it wasn't my eyes I was looking through. Keep reading.

A few years later, Ted came a second time to this group of people. It was a refresher course. We all felt honored that he would make the trip to see us again. (Of course, attendance did cost another "minimal" fee.) Several of us had become quite proficient in these exercises, as a couple of years had passed, and we had practiced diligently. We were excited to show Ted how accomplished we had become.

I don't remember much of this session either, except that as we stood in our rows practicing our positioning, Ted was walking among us making small adjustments to our stances helping us to reach perfection. At the end of the evening, we were sharing what we had experienced as a group. I remember Amy saying that when Ted had walked by her, he touched her forehead to position her head. She shared that when he touched her, she could see a bright white light through her closed eyes, and that a headache she had been suffering from completely disappeared. She thanked him for that.

At the end of our evening, I felt wonderfully blessed and delighted as Tracey approached me and said that Ted was going to be in town for a few days and was wondering if I could give him a ride to the city and show him an aquarium while he was here. What? Me? He wants to hang out with me? Of course, I'll bring him! What an honor!

The last "miraculous" thing that happened that evening was when we were all getting ready to leave. We were by our cars in the parking lot when Tracey needed to make a phone call and realized that her phone was dead...completely dead. Ted took her phone, cupped his hands around it, and pushed some of his "Qi" into it. I kid you not! This phone powered up and stayed on long enough for her to complete her call. We were all utterly amazed!

The next day, I drove to Tracey's to pick up Ted and headed to the city. I felt a little awkward in his presence and wanted to make a good impression. I chose my words carefully, and desperately tried to be someone with whom he would enjoy spending time. I feel like all that flew out the window when I became a little distracted, and BAM! I ran over a curb and gave myself a flat tire. Yeah…that happened. (Wishing I could insert the emoji that has a hand up to the face here.) Watching Ted, in one of his crisp white shirts and pressed pants, climb under my car to see where to put the jack was completely humiliating! But we got through it.

I did have one of the most seemingly amazing experiences while at the aquarium. As I stood in front of the glass that encased a majestic whale, I was in awe of its beauty. It slowly and gracefully swam over and positioned itself directly in front of me. I lifted both my arms and pressed them against the glass as if to give it a hug. It came close and pressed itself to the glass in front of me. If I moved to the right, it did. If I moved to the left, it did. This was spectacular! Even Ted was moved by this experience, and I really didn't want it to end. I had felt such a connection form between us.

After spending a good amount of time with my new whale friend, we started heading to a new exhibit. Ted stopped me in my tracks. He said I should harvest the Qi from the experience. So right there, in the middle of the aquarium, with people coming and going from the very exhibit I was in, I did just that. I stood smack in the middle of the floor, I closed my eyes, and using the technique he had taught me, I harvested the Qi. We stopped for a bite to eat on the way back up from the city, then I dropped him back off at Tracey's. I never saw Ted again.

~ What God wants you to know ~

Qi (Sometimes spelled Chi) is often referred to as the energy force that flows through and gives life to all things. In the metaphysical world it is taught that if you strengthen your "inner Qi" there are not only health, but emotional and spiritual benefits. In an article found on the website: www.gotquestions.org I came across this:

"By definition alone, the idea of chi is not compatible with the Christian faith. A foundational doctrine of Christianity is that God created all things through Jesus (see Genesis 1:1 and John 1:1–4). It is God who gives life, and by God, through Jesus, all things are sustained (see Psalm 147:9 and Colossians 1:16–17).

Some may argue that chi is just a different term for the "life" that God breathed into Adam (Genesis 2:7). But we can't transplant the term chi into the Christian faith because the philosophy behind chi (Taoism) is also incompatible with Christianity. For example, the Taoist view of "God" is that each person has his or her own definition of what "god" is, and each definition is perfectly acceptable—neither right nor wrong. In the Christian faith, God is not defined by people's perceptions. Rather, He reveals who He is to us (see Jeremiah 29:13–14). While God is infinite and beyond full human understanding, He has revealed certain things about Himself and is able to be known personally. In Christianity, Jesus Christ is the only way to a real relationship with God (see John 14:5–7). The idea of chi cannot be separated from the spiritual realm. When one engages with the spiritual realm, he or she will either encounter God or the demonic."

Well said! And furthermore, you can trust me when I tell you that you are not only taking in a harmless "energy" or "Qi" as it is labeled in Qigong, but this is also a demonic spirit that you are welcoming into your flesh. Anything, *any* energy, *any* healing that you are inviting or welcoming into your body that is not done in the Name of Jesus Christ is not of God. But the fact that you are doing this in ignorance, does not keep it/them from entering in. To even make things more complicated, or confusing (and we know that God is NOT the author of this), we are coming into a time where the devil's army will start introducing themselves as "Christ."

For many shall come in my name, saying, I am Christ; and shall deceive many. (Matthew 24:5)

First, I'd like to mention that the Lord Himself said that there would be physicians, so we know that sometimes sickness will be such that we need a Doctor's help. I personally always pray first, in the event the master healer, Jesus Himself, will bring the healing. So, there is nothing wrong with going to a medical physician when needed.

Second, there are instances in the Bible where healing took place outside of a physician's domain. There is an abundance of scriptures that reference healings or deliverance done by Jesus Himself, or by His apostles. Sometimes Jesus brought about the healing by just speaking it. The same way He spoke all of creation into existence. He said it, and it was so.

And behold, there came a leper and worshipped him, say, Lord, if thou wilt, thou canst make me clean. And Jesus put forth his hand, and touched him, saying, I will; be thou clean. And immediately his leprosy was cleansed. (Matthew 8: 2-3)

If His apostles were the vessels used to bring forth the healing, it was done in His name, or for His glory.

And a certain man alme from his mother's womb was carried, whom they laid daily at the gate of the temple,

which is called Beautiful, to ask alms of them that entered
into the temple, who seeing Peter and John about to go into
the temple asked an alms. ... Then Peter said, " Silver and
gold have I none; but such as I have given I thee: In the
name of Jesus Christ of Nazareth rise up and walk. And he
took him by the right hand and lifted him up: and
immediately his feet and ankle bones received strength. And
he is leaping up stood, and walked, and entered with them
into the temple, walking, and leaping, and praising God."
(Acts 3:2-8)

If the name of Jesus wasn't mentioned, people certainly
still knew that the apostles were chosen by the Lord, walked
with the Lord, taught by the Lord, being used by the
Lord…and the Lord received the glory.

And by the hands of the apostles were many signs and
wonders wrought among the people; (and they were all with
one accord in Solomon's porch. And of the rest durst no
man join himself to them; but the people magnified them.
And believers were the more added to the Lord, multitudes
both of men and women.) Insomuch that they brought forth
the sick into the streets and laid them on beds and couches
that at the least the shadow of Peter passing by might
overshadow some of them. There came also a multitude out
of the cities round about unto Jerusalem bringing sick folks,
and them which were vexed with unclean spirits; and they
were healed everyone. (Acts 5: 12-16)

Exercise or stretching in and of itself, is not bad, nor
Ungodly. It is when there is anything spiritual attached to it
that we must use discernment and stay clear.

There is no "grid" of the universe that can be manipulated
through focus nor intent. This was nothing more than another
attempt by the devil to steal God's glory. The demons that
had already begun to possess me at that time were clouding or

masking what I would see with my physical eyes. Sometimes, it was as if I was actually looking through their eyes. Any why not? They were dwelling inside me. As I continued to surrender myself to them, giving them authority over my physical body, I unknowingly gave them power to manipulate my senses. I saw many things over the years as I unsuspectingly served the devil. Some real, maybe some not, but it all certainly seemed real to me at the time.

I wish someone had provoked my thought process at the time with a simple question. Maybe with something like: "What does God's word have to say about what you are seeing or experiencing?" But then again, even God Himself knew that I didn't know His word. And maybe I didn't even believe that the Bible *was* the very Word of God. If someone does not yet have that understanding, shoving the Bible down someone's throat will be to no avail. I thank God for my Pastor and his wife who once I was delivered spent years methodically working their way through the Bible with me. A lesson I pray to remember when ministering to others who are still entrapped in the snares of the fowler.

CHAPTER 5
Yoga

~ What the enemy wanted me to think ~

While I'm on the topic of seemingly innocent exercise, I cannot move forward without mentioning Yoga. While I did not get heavily involved with this, I did "get my toes wet," so to speak. I found that the vast array of people and personalities I met through Yoga had a common thread with myself and the people I met through Qigong. We were all looking for answers. We were looking to find ourselves. To better ourselves. Looking to find out what we were made of, or the purpose we were made for. We were all looking to connect with a higher power. We were looking for healing. All kinds of healing.

Both methods of exercise taught that much of what we were looking for was, in fact, within ourselves. That we not only are able to connect with, or yoke ourselves to, the "Divine," or God, or whatever you were specifically looking for or called it, but that we could develop God-like qualities within ourselves.

There was a type of freedom people found in these modalities. Freedom of expression, love, freedom to "be oneself." And because we were all searching to elevate ourselves to higher plateaus of humanity, it was often said, or we often shared a common belief, that the universe had crossed our paths for a reason. We had been brought together to serve a higher purpose. We felt a connection with each other. I was trying to become a better person, they were trying to become better people, so that formed almost an instantaneous, unspoken bond or kinship with one another. A respect for one another. The connection was real.

While I certainly cannot speak with any great expertise on Yoga, I can talk about what I perceive to be some common knowledge or beliefs about it. There are a variety of practices that are now falling under the umbrella of Yoga. Many are linked to different Indian philosophical systems, and if it is true Yoga, have a basis in Hinduism. As far as I understand it, most Hindus believe in reincarnation. They live many lives as they experience a cycle of death and rebirth. Some believe this rebirth happens immediately after death, while I believe others hold onto the notion that you can go on to exist in another realm. I was taught those same beliefs while in the metaphysical world. Someone at that time went as far as to say that you could choose which body you would like to enter and live in. Sometimes even choosing a body that will ultimately be diagnosed with a terminal illness because that experience was necessary to become complete or whole. With each lifetime, you could accumulate new experiences, wisdom and knowledge, all of which is crucial in developing into "our ultimate selves."

First, Yoga is not just simply exercise. While you certainly can choose to solely partake in the physical aspect of practicing the poses taught, there is most definitely a spiritual side to it. The postures or poses can help you develop muscular strength, become more flexible, burn toxins, and experience the ability for improved balance. It is no secret that while someone is partaking in this, they can also choose to practice entering into deeper states of mediation. On the surface? Yeah, totally exercise, but the philosophy and spirituality of its origin dates back thousands of years.

A sum of what had been explained to me by a variety of people is as follows: that through the discipline of breathing techniques, specific poses, concentration, chanting, and fasting, to name a few things, you can move energy in the body, open and purify the chakras (which I will get into in a future chapter), resulting in purifying one's body, mind, and soul. This ultimately would enable someone to focus for longer periods of meditation leading to higher states of awareness and "being."

There are eight steps (referred to as the 8 Limbs) of Yoga. They are basically guidelines to living a "good" life. Be good. Do good. Feel good.
The first limb deals with ethical standards and integrity.
There are five of them. It was explained in simple terms to me as these are things we should not do.

- Nonviolence
- Truthfulness (we should not lie, nor deceive)
- Non-stealing
- Continence (moderation, self-control)
- Non-covetousness (freedom from greed)

Of course, I would want to be around people who make it a practice to NOT do those things! Who wouldn't, right?

The second limb deals with the things you should do in order to maintain or live an ethical life.

- Cleanliness
- Contentment
- Self-discipline
- Study of sacred scriptures and one's self
- Surrender to God

Again, all good qualities for which to strive! One would certainly think this makes for good people!

The third limb is the actual postures or poses of Yoga. The teachings of Yoga include the view that the body is a temple of spirit. We must care for the spirit that dwells within us in order to spiritually grow. Through the practice of the Yoga poses, we can develop the habit of discipline and the ability to concentrate. Both attributes are particularly important and even necessary for meditation.

The fourth limb has to do with breathing exercises. Yoga teaches that the life force is in the breath, and that our breathing is directly connected to our mind and emotions. That by mastering breathing techniques we can essentially open energy channels to either stimulate or calm ourselves and essentially extend life itself.

As you can see, the first four limbs really focus on refining our personalities and gaining mastery over the body. It is about developing an energetic awareness and is supposed to prepare you for the second half of the Yoga journey which deals with senses, the mind, and ultimately attaining a higher state of consciousness.

The fifth limb has to do with mental concentration or focus. It has been said that by withdrawing from the outside world while simultaneously detaching from our own senses, we can objectively observe the habits that are having a negative influence on our health and interfering with our inner growth. This is usually done by repeating a mantra (a word, sound, or phrase), to clear the mind and strengthen one's ability to concentrate.

The sixth limb in plain terms, is meditation. It is the uninterrupted focus on one thing, or energy source within the body geared to deal with the distractions of the mind itself. The goal is to slow down the thought process, transcend those thoughts, and get to a state where the mind is not constantly thinking thoughts.

The seventh limb is a keen awareness, without specific focus. A person is supposedly able to quiet the mind to where there are little to no thoughts at all.

The eighth, and final limb has been described as the ultimate state of bliss; where the meditator has, in essence, transcended self altogether, and has become one with the universe, or God, or the Divine himself. I have even seen it stated that the individual can experience the peace that passeth all understanding. Some teachings include that we can in essence become God or can come to realize that we already *are* God. Attributes belonging to God alone can be strived for and people supposedly are able to operate in the power and authority that belongs to God alone.

~ What God wants you to know ~

While all of what is stated above seems beneficial in promoting health, wellness, and spiritual development, the Lord desires for me to share some hidden truths that perhaps the enemy of your soul never thought you (or possibly a loved one) would ever find out. I'm going to try to address this paragraph by paragraph for ease of your understanding.

I find it interesting that the first step or limb as it is called, introduces some great human qualities or levels of integrity that we all should follow. I mean, my goodness! They are even Biblical! Oftentimes, when the devil tries to sway us from the Lord's path of holiness and righteousness, he will even seemingly use God's word to do it! That's how he gets us to think "Hmmm...this sounds ok. No harm, no foul here!" Right?

But as soon as we get to the second limb...there it is! Right in the midst of some other clean, profitable ways to live. Study of Sacred scripture and self. There is a scriptural base or foundation to Yoga. I have never read any of it. I did not even research it for the purpose of being well informed for this portion of my book. Some things, I am just unwilling to subject myself to! So, while I cannot comment on this with any prior wisdom or knowledge, I can with certainty say that if it is teaching you how to develop spiritually and it has left Jesus out of the equation, it is not of God! Furthermore, it will most definitely lead you away from your eternal salvation with God. I will back this up 100% by the time you get to the end of this book. I implore you...keep reading!

Some teachers even encourage students to talk about and quote scripture from the Bible. This is again an age-old tactic of the devil. Interjecting some truth into a mix of his lies. Surely, if someone believes in God, and His word, by introducing Biblical scriptures into a practice one could be deceived into thinking the whole practice is of God. But that would be like adding a few drops of red food coloring into a glass of water and expecting only a portion of the liquid to be changed in color. And saying in your mind, "I'll only drink the water that's not tainted." It is impossible.

"A little leaven leaveneth the whole lump."
(Galatians 5:9)

In the second limb, it also talks about the study of one's self. It is totally ok to examine one's self, but the very word of God says we are to do that with a specific intent.

Examine yourselves, whether ye be in the faith; prove your own selves.. (2 Corinthians 13:5)

That is what we are supposed to be looking for within ourselves. Are we in the faith? Faith in Jesus Christ. Are we in alignment with the Lord? With His word? With His Holy Spirit? And I thank God that He doesn't leave it up to us to determine whether or not we are holy or righteous, or perfect in His sight. His word tells us that:

Every way of a man if right in his own eyes; but the LORD pondereth the hearts.
(Proverbs 21:2)

And it is the Lord, Himself, who will reveal to us the things we can't recognize within ourselves, and correct us. All we have to do is seek after His will, His ways, and be open to receiving it when He shares with us what that is.

For whom the Lord loveth he chasteneth, and scourgeth every son whom he receiveth.
(Hebrews 12:6)

The third thing referenced in that second limb is that we must surrender to God. This perhaps is the scariest truth I have come to know. Just because something is referred to as "God," doesn't necessarily mean it is *the* Almighty God, Creator of the Universe, Sustainer of Life, the One, True God! We are getting closer to the day where the Lord Himself opened my eyes to this petrifying truth!

> *...For though there be that are called gods, whether in heaven or in earth, (as there be **gods many**, and **lords many**,) But to us there is but **one God**, the Father, of whom are all things, and we in him, and one Lord Jesus Christ, by whom are all things, and we by him.*
> *(1 Corinthians 8: 5-6)*

Now we come to the third limb, which perhaps is where many people are unknowingly partaking in something that is contrary to the word of God, but very much in alignment with the metaphysical world. With every pose, there is symbolism inherent in its shape. These profound symbols and underlying metaphors are said to bring more magic and meaning with every moment spent in them. The practice of these poses is supposed to be coupled with awareness and intention, and approached with a specific and clear purpose in order to reap the benefits available from them

Without getting into the specific poses, I will share what can supposedly be achieved through the practice of some of them, and what God's word has to say about it.

- A simple positioning of the hands together, leaving a small space in between them allows someone to place an intention or prayer into that space. By holding that space consciously, you can create an avenue for blessings to enter your heart and your life.

The word of God says:

47

Be careful for nothing; but in everything by prayer and supplication with thanksgiving let your requests be made known unto God. (Philippians 4:6) and...

Delight thyself also in the LORD; and he shall give thee the desires of thine heart. (Psalm 37:4) and...

Every good gift and every perfect gift is from above, and cometh down from the Father of lights, with whom is no variableness, neither shadow of turning (James 1:17)

Basically, if we want or need something, we should pray to Jesus for it! If it is good, and profitable, and within His will (which is always perfect), He will grant it! We should most certainly NOT focus our effort, energy, or intent on a space, and allow whatever is to be manifested within that space into our heart, or lives! You literally have no idea to what you are opening yourself!

- Specific poses can help you feel grounded and balanced.

Even if you had personally searched the whole world over, there is absolutely nothing you will ever find that gives you more assurance, strength, peace, love, joy than Jesus! He is the unshakable, immovable rock and foundation that can withstand any storm! Any trial! Any tribulation!

Jesus said:

Whosoever cometh to me, and heareth my sayings, and doeth them, I will shew you to whom he is like: He is like a man which built an house, and digged deep, and laid the foundation on a rock: and when the flood arose, the stream beat vehemently upon that house, and could not shake it; for it was founded upon a rock. (Luke 6: 47-48)

- While holding a certain pose, you are supposed to use your third eye to see the vastness of everything that is available to you. Introducing an all things are possible mindset.

According to Wikipedia, "The third eye is a mystical and esoteric concept of a speculative invisible eye, usually depicted as located on the forehead, which provides perception beyond ordinary sight." While involved in the metaphysical world, I personally had some experience with this. You are basically seeing through a spiritual eye. Question is...what spirit? (We will be getting into the specifics of those spirits in Chapter 8.) And as far as all things are possible, the Bible says:

I can do all things through Christ which strengtheneth me.
(Philippians 4:13) and...

...but with God all things are possible.
(Matthew 19:26) and...

For with God nothing shall be impossible (Luke 1:37)

The thing is all things are possible with God! But even operating outside of Him, you might see things that you would consider to be miraculous. Be not deceived here, the devil does have some power, but certainly not exceeding the power of God! What you need to know is that if you are not approaching the One True God for it, what you receive most likely will not be coming from Him. And trust me on this, if it is not coming from God, there will be payment required. Somehow, some way, but it will be required. The good news? Jesus came to pay the price! If you want Him to step in, He will.

Some other things promised from practicing these poses:

- You can align yourself with nature

I say, why not align or connect yourself with the Creator of nature! If you attempt to connect yourself with nature, mother nature, the universe, etc., there will be something showing up to receive your worship, but it will not be God. You need to call Him by name, and that's Jesus. Ignorance, as I have learned the hard way, won't save you here. What you call on, will respond!

Today, I even find that many Christians now partake in the practice of Yoga. Guys, its root is linked to Hinduism! If you call a tree a flower, it is still a tree!!! God's word says that He will give you the desires of your heart, right? (Psalm 37:4) Do you desire the truth? I mean the real truth? God's truth? Even if it is contrary to what you have been led to believe for a long time? If you are earnestly seeking "the truth," then I believe that the Lord has made a way for this book to make it into your hands.

When I said Jesus came to pay the price, that holds true here, too! While the enemy may have had the initial victory of deceiving you into something that does not line up with God's word or will, God has made a way for you to hear His side of things! Then, it is up to you to:

...Choose you this day whom ye will serve... but as for me and my house, we will serve the Lord.
(Joshua 24:15)

Continuing with things promised or supposably achieved through the practice of Yoga:
- By reaching high, you can connect with the divine.
- You can open your heart to divine connection.
- You can imagine yourself flying between earthly and spiritual planes as you connect with the divine and soar through life's journeys.

I say, if you are reaching to connect with "something"

auspiciously labeled as "divine" but without a specific title (Jesus), you will connect with something that *wants* to be reverenced as divine. But it most certainly won't be.

There are so many more poses, and spiritual connections and promises, but I think I will just leave this here.

The fourth step, or limb, teaches that the life force is in the breath, and that our breathing is directly connected to our mind and emotions. God's word says:

> *For the life of the flesh is in the blood..*
> *(Leviticus 17:11)*

Blood, NOT breath! The devil is a liar!

And as far as needing a calming force for anxiety, depression, nervousness, etc., Jesus is that, too!

> *For unto us a child is born, unto us a son is given; and the government shall be upon his shoulder: and his name shall be called Wonderful, Counsellor, The mighty God, The everlasting Father, **The Prince of Peace**.*
> *(Isaiah 9:6)*

> *For God hath not given us the spirit of fear; but of power, and of love, and of a sound mind.*
> *(2 Timothy 1:7)*

How do we truly tap into all the goodness of God? Keep reading! That comes at the end of the book...it is the best part!

As far as the last four limbs of Yoga, it all has to do with clearing your mind, directing your focus inward on oneself, meditation to slow thoughts to hopefully one day, no thoughts. This all will hopefully get you to the final phase which is to transcend self altogether. To become one with the universe, the divine, god, or whatever higher entity you identify with or are being taught to seek after.

Okay, God never said "clear your mind!" But He did say something quite the opposite!

Be sober, be vigilant; because your adversary the devil, as a roaring lion, walketh about, seeking whom he may devour
(1Peter 5:8)

We are supposed to stay keenly aware and on the lookout! Not emptying our minds, and leaving them wide open for whomever, whatever fancies to fill them!

We are supposed to meditate on the ways and works of God:

I remember the days of old; I meditate on all thy works; I muse on the work of thy hands.
(Psalm 143:5)

We are supposed to meditate on the word of God:

Thy word is a lamp unto my feet, and a light unto my path.
(Psalms 119:105)

The law of the LORD is perfect, converting the soul; the testimony of the LORD is sure, making wise the simple. The statues of the LORD are right, rejoicing the heart: the commandment of the LORD is pure, enlightening the eyes. The fear of the LORD is clean, enduring forever: the judgments of the LORD are true and righteous altogether. More to be desired are they then gold, yea, than much fine gold: sweeter also than honey and the honeycomb. Moreover, by them is thy servant warned; and in keeping of them there is great reward.
(Psalms 19:7-11)

Remember where it stated above that even the practice of Yoga can grant you "the peace that passeth all understanding." Well, well, well! Isn't it just like the devil to use God's own word to lure you into a path that is contrary to God's? For it is God alone who can grant such peace!

Be careful about nothing; but in everything by prayer and supplication with thanksgiving let your requests be made known unto God. And the peace of God, which passeth all understanding, shall keep your hearts and minds through Christ Jesus. (Philippians 4: 6-7)

The devil's intent has and will always be to distract humanity from God's word, God's will, and God's ways. To steal, kill and destroy! And he will make it pretty, attractive to our senses, completely camouflaging it so that we won't know it's leading to our demise. If we were able to recognize its origin, or where it was leading, I have to believe in my heart that we would choose not to follow.

While I did previously state that I am no expert on Yoga, I can say with utmost certainty that I have, however, operated in the Holy Spirit of the Living God, Jesus Christ, to deliver people who had become demonically possessed during the practice of it. I have asked one such individual to share their experience with Yoga. This is her testimony:

"I practiced Yoga very intensively for 25 years. I kind of stumbled into it at a time when I was dealing with a severe depression while also in a graduate program and living on my own. While I eventually did spend about 7 years practicing the Yoga postures, that was a very minor part of it for me. Most of it was meditation, chanting, studying the philosophies on which Yoga is based, and mantra repetition. At the time I was not practicing any religion and had no real relationship with God. Through my practice of Yoga, I felt like I had come to know God in a very intimate way. I felt a joy and peace that I had never known. As I progressed deeper into my study

of Yoga, eventually it became all consuming. It was my entire life. All my friends were from the different Yoga groups I attended, usually 4 to 5 times per week. All my vacations were spent at an ashram where my guru lived during the summers. Eventually, I would have 2 more gurus, be trained as a Hatha Yoga teacher and teach Yoga, travel to India twice, and live in the ashram for 3 years. Everything in my life revolved around my pursuit of Yoga, which I firmly believed was drawing me closer to God and making me a better person. As I continued to practice, I could definitely see myself becoming more mentally clear, calmer, more loving and forgiving. I had an intense desire to know God and would spend hours, in addition to my basic practice of postures, chanting and meditating, researching and studying scriptures to try to understand everything I could and incorporate it into my life. Along the way, I also became involved in various other "new age" practices, including Reiki, channeling, psychic readings. I had many, many spiritual experiences, seeing visions, hearing sounds, that I took as signs that I was progressing along the spiritual path.

I really had no idea that none of this was of God until a conflict developed between me and one of my Yoga teachers that led to me being asked to leave the group. I was completely devastated. I tried to continue the practice on my own, but it was very difficult. Eventually, the Lord reached out to me, leading me to tell my story to a coworker who invited me to his church. I really didn't think I would go but the following Sunday as I was meditating, I had an overwhelming desire to go to his church, and so I went. As soon as I was in the presence of the Holy Spirit that first day, and every time I was at that church, I would be thrown to the ground, and begin coughing, and writhing. When it was explained that I had opened the door to demonic possession by my years of innocently practicing Yoga, many things began to make sense, although I did not want to believe it because I did not want to stop my practice. When I look back over those

25 years and all the experiences I had had, I now see that it was a completely idolatrous system based on Hinduism. I had completely bought into the idea that there were multiple gods and goddesses and bowed down to them. I bowed to and worshipped my gurus, mere human beings. Thinking back on some of the visions I had had, I now see that I was actually seeing demons and welcoming them into my spirit. I really didn't even know that a demonic realm existed so I thought that anything spiritual I saw or heard must be good and must be coming from God. I would never have left Yoga on my own but God saw the true desires of my heart and in His mercy pulled me out and set me on His path of truth and righteousness. When I think back on some of the things I believed, they now seem so obviously false that I don't know how I ever could have believed them. But that is the power of the devil's deception. Many people, even Christians, practice the yogic postures for exercise and justify it by saying that they are not engaged in "the spiritual part." But the truth is that the entire ancient system of Yoga is based on Hinduism and really cannot be separated from it. It is so intertwined. Yoga means to yoke. I thought I was yoking myself to God but was really yoking myself to demonic forces. The purpose of the postures is 2-fold: to strengthen the physical body so that you can sit for longer hours of meditation and attempt to reach higher states of consciousness and union with the divine; and to awaken and purify the energy centers (chakras) in the body so that the Kundalini energy can move from the base of your spine to the crown of your head. We were taught to clear our minds in meditation by focusing on a mantra which we were told meant, "I honor the God within." It actually means "I bow to lord shiva," a Hindu god. When you practice Yoga, you are voluntarily giving your mind and body, and really your spirit, over to forces claiming to be gods but are really demons. I have warned people of the spiritual dangers of Yoga but, unfortunately, there are few who will listen and take it seriously."

So, the truth? Exercise is good! Stretching is good! Just not if it is also linked to a spiritual foundation that is contrary to God's word. So, simply stated, Yoga is not of God. Wait!!! I know this statement might have ruffled some feathers. My hope is that I have not offended you to the point you want to put the book down, I implore you to do your own research when you are ready. It is imperative, for the sake of our souls, that we know the origin of things we are involved with, and to realize there is often more going on behind the scenes of things than we are aware. If you yourself completed a quick search of its origin you would find that the very word "Yoga" means to yoke yourself or create a "union" with the universe, source or god. Small "g"...god. By partaking in it, even though it is in ignorance, you quite possibly are yoking yourself to something. And it is not God.

Jesus said:
"Take my yoke upon you and learn of me; for I am meek and lowly in heart, and ye shall find rest unto your souls."
(Matthew 11:29)

According to God's own word, we are to yoke (join) ourselves to Him. He alone is the Way, the Truth and the Life! (John 14:6) You can only find *your* way, *your* truth, and *your* life in Him! What you are actually looking for, without even possibly knowing it, **IS HIM!**

So, truth be told, whether there is a conscious decision to partake in the spiritual aspect of Yoga or not, the simple practice of it does certainly, unequivocally, open spiritual doors.

CHAPTER 6
Energy Workshops

~ What the enemy wanted me to think ~

Hold on…we are about to go deep. We are at the point in my metaphysical world walk where the devil had pulled me under, completely under, metaphorically and spiritually speaking. If I were making a true reference to being pulled underwater, I would be somewhere at the bottom of an ocean. And by bottom, I mean on an ocean floor, with not enough air in my lungs to even make it a fraction of the way back up to oxygen, light, or life. Oh! But God!!!

Tracey offered her services as a tour guide to Sedona; Arizona, a couple times a year to small groups of people. She made it sound so mystical, so magical. She talked about the healing available in the red rocks of the mountains located there. She talked about the spiritual doors and portals that could be opened for us there. It sounded as if this was the core of the spiritual world. It might realistically be one of the largest gates that is swung wide open to a plethora of spirits waiting to be used by those in the metaphysical world. So I, of course, positively, unequivocally, without a doubt, **had** to go!

At this time, I had recently finished with the chemotherapy, and had gotten a clean bill of health from hepatitis C. I felt surprisingly good, but I was incredibly skinny! You don't eat much when you're nauseous all the time. I was excited that I was done with the treatments, and able to travel. A beloved, dear friend of mine and myself set off on this journey together and were joined by four others; a total of six of us were in attendance for this particular Sedona expedition. The itinerary that Tracey put together for us involved certain activities that we would share and experience as a group, and other things that we could sign up for on an individual basis. I remember the flood of emotions I was experiencing as I was packing; thrilled, elevated, filled with expectation of the possibilities of spiritual enlightenment and awakening that waited for me there.

Tracey had said that we could bring a couple of items (tools that we used in our ministries) to be blessed. I packed absolutely everything that I could fit into my oversized suitcase! Way too many clothes (I don't travel much), some crystals, many crystals, and a tibetin singing bowl. This was a hand-hammered bowl, that when rubbed with its accompanying mallet around the edge would produce a deep tone. The vibrational tone was believed to relieve stress/anxiety and bring healing for all types of sicknesses by supposedly clearing energetic blockages within the body. I used to put the syringe of interferon into this bowl and fill it with "healing vibrations" before Chris injected it into my leg. So, I crammed this bowl and several crystals that I had used for healings (to be talked about in a later chapter) into my bag thinking "if I'm going to continue to use them in my ministry, they should be blessed!"

My suitcase just met the 50 lb. weight limit set by the airport. Whew! Anything over 50 lbs. would have cost additional fees. At that time, additional fees were incurred for exceeding weight limits, not the size of the bag. Upon arrival in Sedona, my dear friend and traveling partner and myself made our way down to the baggage claim area, then outside to the designated area to wait for Tracey. Here, we met up with the other four individuals of our party. Tracey had arrived a day earlier to get everything ready. She pulled up, and we all piled into a minivan. She gave us a brief tour of some beautiful sights on the way to where we were going to stay. I couldn't believe we were there! I was thinking how blessed I was as I gazed upon a world that most certainly held secrets about to be revealed! We were dropped off in our respective places in a beautiful condominium community. We were paired off two to an apartment. Each place was uniquely decorated (as they were all owned by different people), completely furnished and had a full kitchen.

I unpacked, placing my crystals strategically around the apartment, and my Tibetan singing bowl on the coffee table in the living room. I wanted them to not only omit the healing properties I associated with them into the atmosphere (again, to be talked about in a later chapter), but I wanted them to be able to "soak up all this good energy." As soon as we were all done unpacking, we headed to the grocery store so we could stock up on some essentials for the week: coffee, cream, breakfast items, etc. We then headed back to the apartment to get ready for the evening.

Tracey informed us that after a short rest, she would be picking us up. That we were all going out to dinner to kick off our excursion and get to know one another. The restaurant was gorgeous! It was located at the base of those majestic red mountains. The entire wall behind our table was an enormous window that allowed us to bask in the magic of the land.

I remember thinking that while we were all in different places with our spiritual walk and maturity, it seemed that our group was divinely put together at the perfect time for each of us. We knew we would learn much from and with each other, and that somehow this immediate bond that was forming within us was a lasting one.

The next morning, Tracey brought us to a park that had one of the biggest trees I had ever seen standing to greet us at the entrance. I was such a tree-hugger back then, and wasted no time getting my arms around that beautiful, strong specimen. I remember feeling such love, warmth, and gratitude from that tree for the hug I shared. (I know, just wait.) I harvested the "Qi" from that experience and continued down a dirt path that led to trickling brooks and streams lined by flat rocks that welcomed people to sit and enjoy their surroundings.

Wow! This place was truly magical. I remember trying to contain myself but knowing with absolute certainty that during this trip my life was going to be changed forever! And boy was it! Tracey gave us freedom to do as we wished while we were here. Some continued to hike down the paths together, quietly talking with one another. Tracey had shared that this was a "spiritual" site. So, naturally, I wanted to soak up all I possibly could that this place, or the spirits located here, had to offer so I chose some quiet moments alone to practice my "Qigong" on one of those flat rocks. I wanted to internalize, harvest, digest, ...everything. Tracey had said that there was a spiritual aspect or connection to all that was there. The water, the stones in the streams, the flat rocks we were sitting on, the tall grasses, the wind... a sacred place. She attributed a living quality to all things.

Before we left that location, I had bent down to gather a few stones from the stream. (I have always collected rocks.) Tracey told me that I needed to "ask their permission to be taken back with me to New York", which I respectively did. As I slowly searched the waters for the perfect keep-sake stones, I gently picked up the ones that caught my attention. I quietly asked if they would like to come home with me. There was most definitely a presence that washed over me. It was calming, soothing, and beautiful. I took that as a "yes "and took those stones with me. Once in the minivan, Tracey further explained to the group of us that the spiritual connection of all nature was deeply rooted here. That if we wanted to take *anything* from it, we needed to ask its permission to do so. It somehow made sense to me, so I kept that in mind, and obliged throughout the entire journey.

There were many experiences, spiritual encounters during this Arizona trip, but let me get to one of most significance, the one most profound, the one that truly opened all floodgates of the spiritual world for me.

There was a woman who Tracey had contracted with to run

energy workshops over the course of this trip for us to all experience together as a group. We will call her Claire. We always met in Tracey's condo for these sessions. I don't remember specifically how many workshops we attended with Claire, but there were several over the course of a number of days. In the first few, we did some exercises on individual bases, and for some, we paired up in teams. While I did experience "something" during those sessions, it was the last session that we attended with Claire that I want to share with you.

We were all sitting on chairs that had been arranged in a circle. We were instructed to close our eyes and open our minds and ourselves to the experience. Claire started with the person sitting to my left. She was allowing "energies" to flow through her and into him. She moved skillfully, and spoke with a calm, assuring tone. I don't remember what she was saying to him. We were supposed to be collectively open to what was being shared to the group but welcoming on an individual basis what was going to be given or shared with us specifically.

As soon as Claire started this exercise, there was a presence around me that I had never felt before. It wasn't scary, but it was strong. Keeping my eyes closed, I remember seeing a blue sky with clouds. As the exercise went on, I was floating higher and higher toward a light that was beyond the clouds. I thought it was God. How I so wanted to reach him! With each new person that Claire moved to as she made her way around the circle, I drew closer to that light, and the presence became stronger and stronger over and around me. My body started physically moving. Swaying back and forth. It is astounding, as I look back, that I was not frightened, but intrigued.

By the time Claire made her way around the circle to the person sitting on my right, my body was moving with great force. So much so that as soon as she took her hands from that person and held them over me, my body was convulsing with such energy or power, that I no longer could stay on my chair and was somewhat thrown to the floor. I could literally feel this "energy" enter my body, and swirl around inside, causing my body to swirl with it. It might have looked violent, but it didn't feel violent. On the contrary, it felt remarkable.

This session went on for quite a while. My dear friend cried in horror as she observed what was taking place (looking back, she was the only one with an appropriate response), the others just watching in awe and amazement as Claire was used by the "spirit world" to finish imparting spiritual gifts to me. As the exercise ended, I remember being so incredibly close to the light beyond the clouds. But I was "sent back" to complete some work. When all was said and done, I truly had been transformed into a vessel that would be used by many spirits. Clair and Tracey took my dear friend aside and eased her concern. They explained that something beautiful had happened. That I was chosen to experience these things, and that it was not harmful to me, but miraculous. That this was an experience that should be celebrated. She felt better, and we celebrated.

The closeness that I felt to Claire and everyone on this Sedona excursion was unexplainable. We had embarked on a quest together to find something supernatural. And we found it. Together. The next day, we went to a crystal shop. There was a seat within that store that was called a spiritual portal. It was kind of egg-shaped. You could sit inside it and be enveloped in an array of crystals, gemstones, and, of course, all the spirits attached to them. It was a special seat, used to connect to the spirit realm. Not for public use. Tracey, being a frequent visitor to that establishment, got permission for us to try it. We took turns, one by one. Each of us sharing our experience with the rest of the group as we stood up from it. Until it came time for my turn. As soon as I sat down, the same strong, powerful presence started to envelop me. I started moving, swaying, convulsing. Spirits were talking to me! Allowing me to share the atmosphere of the spiritual realm with them! Thinking all the while, this is so cool!

Making my way around the store, I picked up various crystals and immediately "connected" with them. Certain ones would make me feel cold, others warm, others fuzzy minded, others especially clear-minded and focused. Some of our small group were even looking to me to choose the right crystal or gemstone for them to use in their ministries. Wow! Just like that! In an instant! I was enlightened!!!

The last experience from this trip I would like to share with you is the massage that I had signed up for. This was one of the items on Tracey's itinerary that we could choose to partake in. A hands-on energy healer, massage therapist would come to your condo with her services. Of course, my friend and I had to partake in this! Why not indulge in things we don't usually get to do? After all, we deserved it, didn't we? We will call the therapist Rebekah.

Rebekah knocked on the door. We welcomed her in and watched as she set up her massage table and essential oils. Oh, my goodness! So many essential oils! This was yet another time the "spiritual world" had many gifts to impart to me. The massage, coupled with the energy work was supposed to relax my muscles, relieve the stress, and release the energy blockages within my body. For the most part, this was a relaxing experience…until the end of it. After she had methodically kneaded the knots and tensions out of my muscles, she stood at the head of the table. She held her hands a few inches away from the top of my head and proceeded to allow or "channel" energies through her into me. I could feel this energy enter through my head, travel through my body (supposedly cleansing energy sources within my body as it went) and exiting out my feet. The flow of energy became so strong that my body was once again moving, almost convulsing, as things surged through my body, "cleansing" all blockages and negativity from me.

Once done, I asked Rebekah if that was "normal. She said it doesn't happen often, but she had seen it in the past. She said that she had considered herself blessed to be part of the experience. She explained that she could literally see a vast array of colors enter my head, flow through my body, and out my feet. When I tried to stand up, I felt as if I was walking in an astral plane. Like I was floating! Wow again, right?

I took many things home from that trip. One such item was a crystal singing bowl. This singing bowl was on loan to Tracey from a local shop and was in her condo while we were there. One evening, I had some alone time with Tracey. While sharing something troubling I was going through with her, the bowl began to "sing" on its own. No one was rubbing the mallet around the rim of it, no one was touching it! I asked Tracey "Do you hear that?" She said that it was the singing bowl connecting with my grief. It was omitting "healing tones" for me. Wow, right? I went back to my condo that evening somehow longing for that bowl. The group pitched in and bought it. They gave it to me on the last night of our trip while we were out to dinner. I loved this group, and they apparently loved me.

I took many stones back to New York with me. (My suitcase certainly exceeded that 50 lb. weight limit at the airport for my return flight.) One night, I was going through them, admiring them, one by one. When I got to this one small stone that I had taken from the stream mentioned earlier, a cold chill washed over me. Did that really just happen? I put the stone down. I picked it back up, and the same cold chill washed over me once again. It wasn't a good feeling. I called Tracey. She explained that the stone was "unhappy" and longing for its home. I later gave that stone to Tracey. She took it back to Arizona, to the exact stream it came from, on her next excursion there.

What else did I take back? Spirits. Many, oh so many, spirits.

~ What God wants you to know ~

I came across another article on www.gotquestions.org that so simply and eloquently addressed the question: "What does the Bible say about energy healing?"

"Answer: In a world where people are constantly grasping for deeper meaning, deeper spirituality, and a higher purpose, energy healing is one more New Age philosophy that presents itself as very desirable to human beings. Born with sin, we all come into the world with the strong belief that we are the center of the universe—that we are in control of our health, our bodies, our lives, our circumstances, and our destinies. Those who have not turned to God for Truth have no choice but to search for it within themselves.

The practice of energy healing is not in itself a religion, but it is a pathway to one's own spirituality. It leads us on a personal journey that encourages us to focus on ourselves and how our energy is in synch with the energies of the cosmos, the earth, and all other life. Through this, we can supposedly be taught to heal ourselves by using clairvoyance to "visualize" where the negative energy is in order to determine the cause of the problem, whether it is physical, emotional or spiritual.

The use of energy healing encourages us to put our full trust in ourselves and our own bodies, which is a form of worship. For most who participate in energy healing, no recognition is given to the one true God, nor does He receive any praise for healing. The person using these methods of healing has made himself into his own god. Getting involved in energy healing is spiritually dangerous, to say the least.

The Bible tells us that Jesus is the One who came to heal. "Then Jesus said, 'come to me, all of you who are weary and carry heavy burdens, and I will give you rest.'" (Matthew 11:28)(NLT) God does not want or expect us to help ourselves. He is the source of life, of all that is good and true. Those who refuse to acknowledge Jesus will never come to a place of spiritual healing. "For this people's heart has become calloused; they hardly hear with their ears, and they have closed their eyes. Otherwise, they might see with their eyes, hear with their ears, understand with their hearts and turn, and I would heal them. (Matthew 13:15)"(NIV)

The scary thing is most people are in search of God. We all innately desire our Creator, but oftentimes, just don't really know who that is.   Without Biblical teachings and foundations, the very enemy of your soul takes this as an opportunity to introduce himself as God. The devil will take on many forms and use whatever modality he needs to in order to grab your attention and get you to follow him down the deepest rabbit hole possible.

We all need healing. True healing can only come from Jesus! We all desire power. There is no greater power or joy that shines above that of operating in the Holy Spirit for God's glory and the furthering of His Kingdom!

Warning: Know who you are getting a massage from! You may be receiving more than relief for tired, achy muscles! Many massage therapists, even though it is not openly stated, believe in or even partake in energy work without ever mentioning it to their clients. This could even be a simple prayer that they say to themselves before starting. All well-intended, but if a prayer is lifted to "powers that be" or basically anything outside of Jesus, you most certainly are being surrounded and impacted by spirits outside of Jesus! If they believe in Chakras (energy sources within the body; again, I will be addressing this in a future chapter), they most certainly are involving spirits from the metaphysical world. To be clear, these are entities from Satan's army. They may feel beautiful, bring what may appear to be healing, but as you will see, they are NOT beautiful, and the results they bring are devastating.

I will be getting deeper into the spirits that entered me, what they were, and the impact they finally had on me when I get to the chapter about how the Lord opened my eyes to who

I was serving. Keep reading!

CHAPTER 7
Crystal Healings

~ What the enemy wanted me to think ~

The trip to Arizona did truly open many spiritual doors. One door that I gladly walked through, more like stormed through, was the one that led to crystal healings. My experience in that crystal shop back in Sedona was of such profound magnitude that I took it as a sign from God. I thought that He desired to use me in that particular mode of healing. So, of course, I dove in deep here, too! I think Tracey must have had some incredible "crystal" experiences there as well, because during our weekly mediation group sessions, I noticed more and more crystals in her home. Soon, Tracey started acquiring crystals to sell.

One particular Wednesday evening, I walked into Tracey's house and there must have been 50 or 60 new crystals there. Every single windowsill and flat surface in her home, including her entire kitchen table, was filled with them. I thought that the energy in the house that night was amazing! They were for the most part all clear quartz, but in all different shapes and sizes. Most of them had been cut so that they had flat bottoms, then jutted up in the most amazing natural pointed peaks. Some were pointed on both ends. They looked like magical mountains, and I thought that surely, they held mystical properties. Many of them "spoke" to me. I could feel their energy as I picked them up and couldn't wait to add them to my collection. The amount of money I had spent on them was absolutely ridiculous!

The people in our meditation group received what they needed from these stones in different ways. I remember one girl said she would actually hear them talk to her. That they had a voice! There was a large crystal in Tracey's collection that she had discussed purchasing. Before the evening was over, someone else stepped in and bought it. She said that the crystal was literally screaming at her that it was supposed to have gone with *her*! It belonged in *her* home! It was yelling it to her over and over, incessantly! If she moved to the other side of the room, it yelled louder! It became such an overwhelming experience for her that she had to leave. I remember the look on her face as she left in such haste, literally running out the front door! Now, while this didn't sound pleasant at all, I found myself longing for the gift she had. She could have full on conversations with the stones. I was thinking that had meant a stone could specifically direct her in what needed to be done! It could tell her where healing needed to take place within someone's body! Bizarre, right? I wanted to be able to receive directions like that and help people at a higher level!

Crystals became somewhat of an obsession for me. Each time I held one, I would open myself up to the energies of it. If "it" ministered to me, if I felt something, I would know that it was supposed to come home with me and that it had a specific purpose in my ministry. But that was only the beginning.

Shortly thereafter, Tracey started offering workshops to teach us how to effectively use the crystals to their full potential. There was quite a transformation that took place for me here that impacted me personally, and all those who came to me for healings. What we learned was how to not only receive the energies from the stones, but how to become a conduit for them. We learned how to channel energies through the stones, so that the properties of it could be passed along to the person in need of them. There was a process to this.

First, there was the discerning of what kind of healing was needed and where that was specifically located in someone's body. Then, we needed to decide what type of gemstone or crystal was required. I was taught that each type of stone had a different healing or spiritual property. One was for clearing negative energy, one was to help astral traveling, (Yup! Someone could supposedly travel among the cosmos!), one helped open pathways so that you could channel spirits (I'll talk about that in an upcoming chapter). Absolutely any attribute of your own being whether it be physical, emotional or spiritual that was lacking or in need of healing, could be obtained or replenished from a gemstone.

Some attributes that people came to me for crystal healings included:

Grounding, nourishment, stability, empowerment, hope, joy, truth, harmony, peace, warmth, wellbeing, nurturing, protection, cleansing, intuition, healing from grief, wisdom, communication, vitality, confidence, optimism, vision, insight, learning, purification, courage, sexuality, perspective, contentment, love, psychic abilities, spiritual awakening, journeying, surrender, and this literally is only naming a few. Whatever you can think of, I was taught it could be obtained from a stone. Can you imagine the collection I had? I wanted to be well equipped to help people with whatever they needed!

Once we identified what type of healing was needed, these workshops taught me that I could use these gemstones or crystals one of three ways. One, you could hold the stone over the area needing healing and allow the stone to do its thing. Two, you could allow your own energies to flow through and "partner" with the healing properties of the stone, and then enter the individual. The third way was to surround yourself with that white, "protective" light I spoke about earlier. We would call upon those powers/principalities, gods/goddesses, the universe, etc., and allow those entities to flow through the crystals/gemstones, bind with the properties of the stone, and then flow into the person needing healing. That was usually my method of choice.

These crystal workshops led to fellowship with a whole new community of people who were also like minded with hearts and intentions to bring healing to a hurting world. I became rather close with someone in particular. We will call him Jesse, Crystal Jesse. I felt like we were instantly family. A long-lost brother or cousin or something. Jesse always had a plethora of crystals for sale. He often toted them around in the back of his station wagon, and he himself offered workshops to help us become familiar with the different properties of crystals and gemstones.

One evening, I met Crystal Jesse in a parking lot. He said he had some new inventory that he wanted to show me. We sat for hours as he handed me crystal after crystal from this new collection he had recently obtained. I remember how happy I was when he exclaimed: "Wow Crystal! You're going to literally blow the roof off my car with all the energy that's flowing through you!" I thought that he was one of the most "gifted" individuals; filled with so much insight, wisdom and knowledge of this crystal world. I felt blessed and fortunate that he was willing to share what he knew with me. Many of the crystals I got from Crystal Jesse became my "go-to's" for healing.

The memories of some of these healing sessions are suddenly extremely vivid. I believe that once again, the Lord is bringing them to my remembrance for your benefit. I am praying that it gives you insight into my heart and intentions at that time, enabling you to identify with those involved with this modality of healing today. There are numerous people who still, as I once did, believe that they are blessed with spiritual "crystal healing gifts." They are beautiful people with good intentions, but their efforts to help humanity are swayed and misguided in complete ignorance. I believe that the Lord created them with compassionate hearts and a desire to be used to heal people. However, without the knowledge of God's word, the devil has swayed them onto a parallel path from the one God had intended for them. I believe that the Lord had desired to be glorified in them, and through them. He receives *no* glory from these "crystal healings," and unfortunately, in innocence, these people are being led further and further away from God's Heavenly Kingdom.

The whole corner of my basement had been partitioned off. The walls were draped in purple satin material. I had a small bookshelf and many tiny shelves fastened to the walls holding my vast array of crystals and gemstones so that they were easily accessible during my "healing sessions." Oh! And I had little white "fairy lights "everywhere!

I always set the ambiance in my room downstairs with candles, incense, music and prayer. I needed to pray! I knew that the "miracles" and "healings" I was seeing were not coming directly from me, and I wanted to keep being used by the powerful forces that allowed me to be part of such mending and restoration! I prayed that these "powers that be" continued to protect me from the sickness that was being healed and that I would continue to see them move in miraculous ways. While I even called on whatever I was calling on at the moment, I believed God was over it all, orchestrating it all. (He wasn't…keep reading.)

I would have the person who came for healing lie down on a massage table that I had set up. After praying, I would run my hands over their body, staying about two inches above them. My hand would typically get warm when I was supposedly over an area that needed healing, whether it be a bone, muscle, or organ. I would let the person know where my hands were over, and more times than not, they would confirm that that exact spot was where their pain was emanating from.

I would then grab the appropriate crystal. Now, I know what I am about to share with you sounds farfetched (as if none of this was so far), but this is literally what I saw! Where my hands became warm, I would see a darkened spot. I believed that this was how the sickness, illness, or disease was being manifested to me so that I could heal it. As I previously mentioned, I would usually use the third approach of the healing techniques I shared above. Why not let the higher powers do what I know I could not? After praying, that white protective light that I surrounded myself with would start to funnel into one pointed end of the crystal, and then stream out the other pointed end in a beam of "healing light." I would start at the outer ring of that darkened spot, and slowly, in a circular motion, go smaller and smaller with that beam of light until the dark spot was gone. At this point, the person would generally exclaim that their pain was gone! Just like that! People who could barely walk into my house because of excruciating pain were jumping up in celebration and awe. Pain free!

People would come to me with all kinds of ailments. Crippling back pain would disappear. Some came with diagnosed diseases and would appear to be symptom-free after a session. People came with tumors that were seemingly gone after a healing session. Some came with digestive issues, joint pain…you name it, people came with it! There are many, many, many scenarios (what I thought were miraculous healings) that I did experience over the years, but you get the gist. Now let's get to what *really* matters!

~ What God wants you to know ~

While I truly never met anyone in the crystal workshops who had any other intention than to bring healing to hurting people, the Lord's word is true and undisputed. Crystal healings are not in alignment with it. But the fact of the matter is that the most well-intentioned, loving people, can be deceived by the enemy of our souls and used in this modality to compound spiritual problems into bigger ones than someone may have initially started with. I have much to share here, let me backup, and start with the crystals and gemstones themselves.

First, crystals are certainly beautiful! Of course, they are! God created them to be beautiful, and they are listed as part of His glorious designs several places in His word. In the book of Exodus, the Lord instructs Moses to create priestly garments for Aaron to wear. They included the placement of specific gemstones.

*And thou shalt take **two onyx stones**, and grave on them the names of the children of Israel: Six of their names on one stone, and the other six names of the rest on the other stone, according to their birth. With the work of an engraver in stone like the engravings of a signet, shalt thou engrave the two stones with the names of the children of Israel; thou shalt make them to be set in ouches (settings) of gold. And thou shalt put the two stones upon the shoulders of the ephod for stones of memorial unto the children of Israel; and Aaron shall bear their names before the Lord upon his two shoulders for a memorial. (Exodus 28: 9-12)*

Moses was also instructed to have a breastplate of judgment made for Aaron to wear:
*And thou shalt make the breastplate of judgment with cunning work; after the work of the ephod, thou shalt make it; of gold, of blue, and of purple, and of scarlet, and of fine twined linen, shalt thou make it. Foursquare it shall be being doubled; a span shall be the length thereof, and a span shall be the breadth thereof. And thou shalt set in its settings of stone, even **four rows of stones**: the first row shall be a **sardius, a topaz, and a carbuncle**: this shall be the first row. And the second row shall be an **emerald, a sapphire, and a diamond**. And the third row a **ligure, an agate, and an amethyst**. And the fourth row a **beryl, and an onyx, and a jasper:** they shall be set in gold in their enclosings. And the stones shall be with the names of the children of Israel, twelve, according to their names, like the engravings of a signet; everyone with his name shall they be according to the*

74

twelve tribes.
(Exodus 28:15-21)

And Aaron shall bear the names of the children of Israel in
the breastplate of judgment upon his heart, when he goeth in
unto the holy place, for a memorial before the LORD
continually. (Exodus 28: 29)

These garments were holy and created for a priest to wear
before the Lord, God Almighty! Isn't it just like the devil to
take something that was meant for a beautiful memorial
before the Lord and to try to steal it for his own glory? The
devil desires to use these crystals and gemstones to build his
kingdom, because portions of God's heavenly Kingdom will
be constructed out of them as is shown to us in the book of
Revelation.

And he carried me away in the spirit to a great and high
mountain, and shewed me that great city, the holy
Jerusalem, descending out of heaven from God, Having the
*glory of God: and her light was like unto a **stone most***
***precious, even like a jasper stone, clear as crystal**...*
(Revelation 21:10-11)

*And the building of the wall of it was of **jasper;** and the city*
*was **pure gold**, like unto clear glass. And the foundations of*
*the wall of the city were garnished with all manner of **precious***
***stones**. The first foundation was **jasper**; the second, **sapphire**;*
*the third, a **chalcedony**; the fourth, an **emerald**; the fifth,*
***sardonyx**; the sixth, **sardius**; the seventh, **chrysolyte**; the*
*eighth, **beryl**; the ninth, a **topaz**; the tenth, a **chrysoprasus**;*
*the eleventh, a **jacinth**; the twelfth, an **amethyst**. And the*
*twelve gates were twelve **pearls**; every several gateswere of*
*one pearl; and the street of the city was **pure gold**, as it were*
transparent glass. (Revelation 21:18-21)

The use of these precious stones for healing is most certainly linked to the occult. I have seen it stated where the very word "occult" means "hidden." Interesting...hidden. When Jesus was crucified on the cross, He said:

"Father, forgive them; for they know not what they do."
(Luke 23:34)

Often, we truly don't know what we are doing, or exactly what we've gotten ourselves involved in, because the root or foundation on which they are built is intentionally "hidden" from us. Isn't that just another definition of being deceived? If the devil can use any of the modalities, I am discussing in this book to deceive us into thinking it's a "good thing," or that we are helping/healing people, then, he's won the fight. Good news...He has NOT won the battle!

Fact number two. Crystals cannot speak; however, the spirits that use them as a place of habitation, can. Why would a spirit inhabit a crystal or gemstone? To receive the praise or glory for the god-like quality that we are attributing to that stone, and you have just partaken in idol worship. So, think about this. If we are holding a stone or wearing a crystal for healing or protection, we are in essence opening ourselves up to receive something from a spirit. This is not the Holy Spirit of the Living God! Nor are these spirits sent by God. And ANY spirit that is not God's, or sent by God, is not OF God. While they may deceive you into thinking that there is a positive result stemming from a crystal...it is a temporary apparition. If you are looking for protection, this spirit can give you a false sense of security. Believe it or not, this would also hold true if you are keeping or holding a cross believing there is protection or healing emanating from it. Protection comes from our Savior directly. The One who died *on* the cross, not the metal or wooden cross itself. In the same vein of thought, this also holds true for any angelic statues, statues of Mary or Saints, we attribute protection (or any God-like qualities) to. I pray that the Lord opens the spiritual eyes of His people, like He did mine. If humanity could only see what they are really surrounding themselves with when they do this. Remember the devil can array himself as an angel of light. When he manifests himself as such, he may look pretty, but trust me again, when the smoke clears...he is anything but pretty.

When I would funnel that white light through a crystal and aimed that beam of light into a person, it wasn't healing them. I was being used by the devil to possess people with demonic entities feigning themselves as good or healing energies. How do I know this with certainty? You'll see. And, trust me, I have repented deeply for this. So, are you wondering why ailments and symptoms would magically disappear? It is because they were merely spirits of infirmity. You see such a spirit referenced in the Bible:

And behold, there was a woman which had a spirit of infirmity eighteen years, and was bowed together, and could in no wise lift up herself. (Luke 13:11)

When another demonic force was brought onto the scene through these healing sessions of mine, that initial spirit would "play dead." By that I mean it would pretend to be dormant, showing no ill effects. If you think that you are healed, or delivered, you will no longer seek to be healed or delivered. This results in a nice, lasting, cozy home or host for that initial spirit which is now joined by one or more spirits. If you are possessed by demonic entities, whose kingdom do you think you will be spending eternity in? Let that soak in.

According to the KJV Dictionary, the definition of possessed is:

"To have the just and legal title, ownership or property of a thing; to own; to hold the title of as the rightful proprietor, or to hold both the title and the thing."

If you are possessed by a devil, owned by a devil, the day you breathe your last, it would have to hold true that you would, in fact, be spending eternity *with* the devil. But if there is still breath in your lungs, there is still time, and thank God for the delivering power of His Holy Spirit!

CHAPTER 8
Channeling Spirits & Spirit Guides

~ What the enemy wanted me to think ~

Okay, here we go. Back to those weekly meditation sessions. Because of what I experienced during those sessions, I longed to operate in the same level of spirituality that Tracey did. We all did! Any why not? Were not messages being given from a realm beyond ours? Was not what was being shared only attainable in this type of setting? After all, the spirits that were flowing and speaking through Tracey were sharing things that could not be seen or heard on the physical earthly plane in which we live. We were taught that you had to enter this spiritual plane to obtain spiritual knowledge. Of course, where there is a demand, there will be a supply.

So, Tracey started introducing workshops to teach the magical skill of connecting with our spirit guides, and then to ultimately channel them. To connect with them meant that you had broken through the barrier that separates the physical from the spiritual plane. That now you could hear and receive messages from the spirit world. To channel them meant that, well, you have reached a pretty high level in your spiritual walk! You in essence would step aside within your body, and allow that spirit to step into it, and use it as a vessel to speak and operate through it. In the eyes of those who gathered each week, this was an amazing gift!

We were taught that each and every person was assigned a spirit guide. This spirit was always with you, guiding, protecting, leading, etc. To connect with them would mean that you were tapping into all the information they held. They could explain to you the things that only they could see, keeping you from traps and pitfalls. They could navigate your every step so that it would be in a positive direction and bring about positive results. Not only that, but they could connect with other spirits, so you had a vast array of info at your disposal.

I remember in vivid detail the first workshop I attended on this. We all were instructed to find a partner and get comfortable. My partner and I chose a spot on the floor. Tracey led us in a meditative prayer. We called upon the usual entities (gods, goddesses, the universe, powers that be) surrounding ourselves with the white light "of protection" that manifested in response to the prayer. Well, this has got to be good, right? After all, we were covering ourselves in prayer! We were asking for protection against anything evil that may want to intrude on this beautiful, magical experience. Hmmm...we'll just see about that.

The atmosphere was most certainly shifting or changing in that living room that day. There was a kind of thickness or presence to it. I could feel it. We were supposed to clear our minds and be "open" to messages that we were going to be receiving from our spirit guides meant for the person with whom we were partnered. I did receive something. The best way I could describe it was that information was downloaded into my mind, but it was kind of vague and muddled that day. (Clarity did increase as time/years went by.) The less I was inhibited to share, the more I received, but it still wasn't very precise. I don't remember at this time any specifics of what I had received, but I do remember it made sense to my partner, and they were grateful for the information. They, in turn, shared information with me for which I was also grateful.

Remember earlier in this book, back in Chapter 4, I mentioned my dear friend Amy and her spirit guide? Well, it was at this particular workshop where I first witnessed her encountering that spirit. It wasn't pleasant for her...at all. Although I was partnered with someone else that day, Amy was sitting on the floor directly on my left. As the rest of us were experiencing something we labeled as "insightful," even "joyous or euphoric," Amy was petrified and burst into tears. None of us on the floor next to her knew what was going on and didn't know what to do, or how to console her, or even if we should intervene to try to console her in fear of interrupting the "connection."

Finally, Tracey came over and talked with her quietly so as to not interrupt what other people were experiencing or receiving. I stopped focusing on my partner and intently listened to what Tracey was saying to Amy. You see, oddly enough, even as this was obviously not "joyous or euphoric" for her, I still longed for the strong connection she seemed to have with that spirit. Amy was explaining that the presence of it was too strong for her. I think (I may be wrong here) that she described him as an American Indian. Very big. Very strong. Very forceful. The experience was overbearing and uncomfortable. But what still made it enticing to me was that she could hear every word he said. As clear as day. It was like having a companion with you every moment of every day. Someone to walk with, talk with, commune with. Someone who could see ahead and give clear and concise directions. Someone who had your back, protecting you from things even coming up behind you. In my mind, it would be okay if that spirit were a little strong…that meant it could be strong on my behalf.

Tracey spent several minutes with Amy explaining to her that she was just not "used to" his presence and that it would get easier over time to connect with it without such discomfort. Amy calmed down and stopped crying. She was eager to get to that place because she had explained that this spirit had been with her for a long time, years. She had come to this workshop in hopes of identifying what/who it was and was looking forward to getting to a place where she did not need to walk around in fear of it. Looking back…oh my goodness! There is something already so, so, so very wrong with this picture!

After countless workshops, and additional hours spent on my own, I did connect with and eventually channel my own "spirit guide." She called herself Margarite. Channeling happened exactly how I explained it above. I could literally feel myself move over inside my physical body shell, and she would "fill up the room" I left inside. While channeling, I completely surrendered the use of my body to her. And she did take over! Even my facial features would transform as she manifested her own appearance. There are many who can testify to this, including my own daughters who saw this take place on numerous occasions. Looking back, I, of course, deeply regret that I ever exposed them to such a thing. Margarite spoke with an accent. I was fully aware of everything she was doing and saying but was like a spectator during these moments. She would talk about things that I had no knowledge of, hence, I and the people who came for readings, thought this information was coming from a higher place and that the whole thing was pretty cool! It never felt scary or uncomfortable. Margarite seemed kind and compassionate. She seemed grateful to have a willing vessel to use so that she could bring comfort and guidance to those who needed it. I was grateful that I had matured enough spiritually to allow this to happen and be lucky enough to witness the "blessings" she bestowed upon people. And besides, I could take back control of my body any time I wanted to…until one day, I couldn't. Keep reading.

Another method of channeling that was taught to me (and of course I practiced it willingly), was called gazing. This was linked directly with discerning someone's "past-lives." People who would want to know who they were, or what they did in past lives, would come to me for a gazing session. I would also offer to do these over the phone as a person did not have to be present for me to connect with their "history."

I would typically sit on the end of my bed and stare or "gaze" into a large mirror located on the wall directly in front of me. Slowly, my own image would become a little "fuzzy" and it would somehow morph into someone completely different. Once I saw a woman's head separate from her body. Just ever so slowly float upward, disconnecting from her shoulders. Oh! I exclaimed! You were beheaded! For some reason, that made complete sense to the individual waiting for an explanation on the other side of the phone line. "That's why I experience all the neck pain I currently suffer with," was their response.

We were taught that once we had identified a pain linked to a past life, we could pray, use the techniques used in "energy healing," and release that pain into the "white light of protection" to be carried away. I prayed with that individual that day. The pain left, and I chalked it up to another successful session. I saw various figures over the years while gazing. Dressed in the garb of different eras of time. Each with such detail! I didn't even know my history enough to manifest these outfits to the extent that I saw. I was once again a spectator. It was like watching a movie play out in the mirror in front of me.

If people were coming to me in person, although they were sitting right next to me, they were unable to see what I saw. There was one instance, however, they certainly felt what I felt. Someone had come asking me to use this technique to try to touch base with the spirit of someone who was still living but had basically "fallen off the face of the earth." It was someone she had become awfully close with and all of a suddenly couldn't get in touch with him. She was worried.

As I started to focus, I saw a boat. I explained that I thought he might be in trouble on a boat. As soon as I had stated that, it felt like we were both being tossed to and fro while on a small boat in the midst of a storm. Our bodies were moving in unison with each other. As if we were sitting right next to each other on this boat, experiencing the same thing at the same time! At some points, it was even difficult to stay seated! We prayed for his safety. I never did hear what happened to that guy.

~ What God wants you to know ~

There is an innate desire within each of us (whether we recognize it as such or not) to be reconnected with our Creator. We all (I believe), regardless of what we call it, recognize that there is something higher, more powerful than us. The Lord, Jesus Christ, is the one above all! Creator of all! Good and evil! He reigns over every power and principality! I pray that you find comfort in the fact that it is HE who desires to be your comforter, companion, and friend. HE desires to bless you with all the wisdom, knowledge and understanding of every circumstance or situation. He reigns supreme over those entities who claim to hold such power!!!

But the Comforter, which is the Holy Ghost, whom the Father will send in my name, he shall teach you all things, and bring all things to your remembrance, whatsoever I have said unto you. (John 14:26)

I will not leave you comfortless: I will come to you. (John 14:18)

Jesus loves you with a love that is greater than all others! He considers us "friends."

Greater love has no one than this, that someone lay down his life for his friends. (John 15:13)

His word tells us that *if* we seek Him, acknowledge Him, He *will* be the one to direct us:

Trust in the LORD with all thine heart; and lean not unto thine own understanding. In all thy ways acknowledge him, and he shall direct thy paths. (Proverbs 3:5-6)

If we ask anyone but Jesus, the information or direction you receive is not coming from the Highest Authority and is less than perfect! Furthermore, regardless of how "on point" or "accurate" that information may seem to be, or how it seems to benefit you to begin with, it is NOT leading you on the path that leads to ultimate victory. That path is God's, and God's alone!

Let me address the notion that there are past lives. The Bible, which is the ultimate authority over life as it was written by the One who created it, says:

And as it is appointed unto men once to die, but after this the judgment (Hebrews 9:27)

Think about it. Why would the devil want you to think that you could live numerous lives? Really, think about that for a moment... if he can get you to believe you have an abundance of lives, many chances to get "it" right, there is no real pressure for you to do good, be good, or get "it" right during this one. After falling or failing, the mentality could easily be "Oh well! I'll get it next time around." Someone with this mindset might often choose to just let things play out as they are, call it "quits" assuming they will get another go-around.

Listen guys, we all fall, many times.

For all have sinned, and come short of the glory of God (Romans 3:23)

But this merciful Jesus is just to forgive and has outstretched arms; waiting to pull us back up. Every time! The thing is, we have this lifetime to get it right! To get ourselves cleaned up and ready for His 2nd coming. He is coming back for His church. A Holy Church! Of course, the enemy of your soul does not want you to know this, because if you're not ready when He comes, you don't go with Him! There is no "late bus" for you to catch like when you were back in school if you missed the first one. And if you die before getting yourself ready, then, unfortunately, you die in your sin. You do not make it then either. How do we prepare? That is in the last chapter. We still have much to go through before we get there. Remember, this was a 13-year journey you are sharing with me.

Let's address the channeling thing. I hope by now that you have surmised this was not a good thing, but I'll go over it just the same. When you allow a spirit to enter your body, you've basically given up ownership and the authority of your body to that spirit. It now possesses you. Owns you. If you think it is a lovely or positive thing, you've obviously not seen what it looks like when that spirit is asked to leave. As discussed in the last chapter, if I am owned by something, other than Jesus, I am going to spend eternity with that something...not Jesus. And just to be clear, the dwelling place of that thing would be Hell.

And now, let's shine the light of the Lord into the darkness called gazing. Basically, as I was now possessed with a plethora of spirits, I was seeing what they manifested before me. I guess I was kind of looking through their eyes. It is the only way I can explain what I saw. And the only reason I have gone into such detail with these memories for you is because you, or someone you know, needs to understand that just because you are able to achieve a "heightened sense of spirituality," experiencing something, or seeing something "in this spirit world," it is not necessarily a good thing. Don't get me wrong here...this is real! You see things that don't seem harmful! You feel things that seem wondrous! It is physically happening to you! And people may even seem to benefit from this all at the time, but ultimately, what you are doing is hurting yourself and them. You are allowing the devil to use you, opening yourself up to demonic possession. You are hurting them also, by holding open a demonic spiritual door for them to be accessed as well.

You know what the amazing thing here is? All that I have explained here feigns in the light and power I have experienced in the Holy Ghost of the Living God, Jesus Christ! Jesus has given gifts to His church. There are gifts of wisdom, knowledge, and prophecy, to name a few! The difference here is that the Lord always has your best interest at heart. He will lead and guide you safely. And His path will ALWAYS lead to His Kingdom!

CHAPTER 9
Divining Rods

~ What the enemy wanted me to think ~

At one particular Wednesday evening meditation group, I met a man we will call Jack. He had never attended a previous session, but he and Tracey were obviously close. I remember thinking as he walked in and took a seat on the window bench next to Tracey that there is something I admire about this man. I knew right away that he had something to share with the group that night...and boy! Did he! I don't remember the specific message, but I do remember we were all blown away, and it was obvious that he had a direct connection to the spirit world.

Jack called himself a seer. Meaning, he could see into the spiritual world, see into the future, see beyond what a person's natural physical eyes could see. He talked with such authority and wisdom; he immediately captivated all who were present that evening. Yet, he emanated grace, kindness, and compassion. There was a certain gentleness that drew me to him. Later I learned that he was a professor at a local college; hence the "teacher" spirit that I would soon come to know and love in him. Jack would actually become the person whom I would respect most in this metaphysical world.

After he had attended a few Wednesday sessions with us, I think it was safe to say that we all admired him and wanted to learn from him. One evening, he brought divining (dowsing) rods to the group. According to Wikipedia: "Dowsing is a type of divination employed in attempts to locate ground water, buried metals or ores, gemstones, oil, gravesites, malign 'earth vibrations' and many other objects and materials without the use of a scientific apparatus." I have also seen the process of finding water with these apparatuses called water witching or water dowsing. I believe divining rods were derived from the original pattern of a forked rod or stick that have been used for centuries.

Jack had made his rods out of ordinary iron hangers. They were straightened, then bent a few inches from one end resembling long "Ls." He had shared with us that he himself had in fact used his divining rods to find underground water. That he merely held them in his hand, and when he came upon a place where there was water underneath the ground, the rods automatically pointed downward. He said that with all his strength he could not lift the tips of his rods back upward nor could the person who was walking with him that day. He then began using his rods for much more than finding water; he used them to decipher information from the spirit realm. He asked if any of us would be interested in attending a workshop on this. There was a resounding "yes" from all who were there. In my mind, any tool that allows me to correctly receive information from the spirit world, is a tool I need in my arsenal.

The workshop took place on a cloudy Saturday morning. I remember pulling up to a store front property in a strip mall. I entered the establishment with great excitement and in anticipation of a new spiritual door about to be opened. It was a large room. I think perhaps it was some sort of exercise facility as there were a lot of mirrors lining the walls. There were long tables in half of the room, with a lot of open floor space in the other. We sat at the tables while Jack introduced us to the philosophy behind the rods. He walked us through a questioning process that we would be using in order to obtain information from the spirits that would be joining us that day. The first half of the morning was spent in this classroom-like forum.

Then, it came to the hands-on portion of the workshop. Jack had fashioned a pile of these divining rods out of hangers.

They were all in a pile in the front of the room, we were each instructed to go pick out two for ourselves. Me, in my usual fashion, took quite some time in picking mine out. They had to be perfect! (They were all exactly the same, but you know! lol)

Once we had our rods, we were asked to go stand in front of the walls of the room. We were to face the wall, and back up several feet. We were to hold the small end of the rods in our hands, pointing the long ends at the wall. Jack taught us the format of a questioning process. It was such that we were supposed to, through a process of elimination, get to the information or answers we were seeking. Following that format, we each asked a question and started walking slowly to the wall. The rods were supposed to move within our grasp in response to what we had asked. I, myself, asked a question, and took a step forward. Both the rods in my hands immediately swung outward! My heart started pounding! I dropped my arms, backed up, lifted my arms again pointing the rods toward the wall. I repeated my question and took a step. Again! Both rods immediately swung outward! What? Could it really be that easy? I looked around the room; not everyone was having immediate success with this, but several were. Jack took his time, coaching each one of us, until we were all victorious in operating our rods. I thought this was absolutely extraordinary! A whole roomful of us now equipped with new tools for our ministries. And we all were using them somewhat skillfully after just one training session!

(Side note: Just because something is labeled "a ministry", does not mean that it is a Christian one, or even of God. This term is loosely, and often, used outside of The Church; perhaps even by the name, luring people into things in which they have no business partaking. Beware, lest even the elect are deceived!)

Crystal Jesse was also at that workshop. He, too, had great success with his rods. After class, we sat and shared our experiences. Of course, he had brought some new crystals with him, including the biggest piece of a crystal called selenite that I had ever seen. This was used to activate intellect and higher consciousness. It was used for enlightenment and spiritual growth. It was about a foot long, was white, and it was beautiful! He placed it on the table in front of me. I laid my hands on it and felt a surge of energy course through me. It wasn't a strong, scary thing...it was light, uplifting, and I felt it was accomplishing precisely what it was supposed to. Enlightening me. I, of course, bought it! From that day forward, I used that crystal in all the psychic readings I did. I usually placed it on the floor under the table I was sitting at and rested my feet on it. It was something that immediately "connected me to the spirit world" ...every time.

As that workshop came to a close, we hugged one another and said our goodbyes. We always hugged one another. As I stated in the beginning of this book, there was a comradery between us. A closeness. A bond, of which Jack was now a part. He seemed well pleased with the results of this get-together and told us he would be putting together another one soon. We were all happy to hear that and eagerly looked forward to the next session.

I introduced these rods into my psychic reading sessions. I thought they were extremely helpful in obtaining answers to specific questions being asked. Though there was one dear friend of mine who didn't like them...at all! We will call her Dot. I met Dot when I first started doing psychic readings. My husband actually went into a law office she worked in and gave her one of my business cards. We seemed to connect immediately and became close friends. She believed in my psychic abilities and quickly became involved and successful in helping me build my customer base. She showed me how to create chat rooms on the computer, where groups of people would sign on and join in the conversation. Dot would act as the moderator of the chat room. She made sure people joining in were added to a list, enabling me to answer the questions of people in the order they signed on. (Though, if I remember correctly, it was all done through typing. No voice, and certainly no video access. This was "back in the day" lol.)

Getting back to the divining rods. Whether Dot was in the room with me, or talking on the phone, she could hear a specific sound whenever I used those rods. She said it was like she could hear them cutting through the air. (What I am imagining here is the sound a lightsaber would make from the Star Wars movies as it was swished through the air, but more metallic.) She hated that sound! It made her uneasy. I myself never heard it. Sometimes, she would call and ask me a question. I would pick up the rods without telling her. She always knew. She'd say, "Crystal, are you using those stupid rods again? I can hear them, you know!" I miss Dot. She has since passed away, but you will hear more about her later in the book.

~ What God wants you to know ~

The use of divining rods seems harmless enough, but the truth of the matter is that the people using them know that the power locating the water, object, or information does not dwell within the rods or sticks themselves. They acknowledge that these are just tools used to tap into a "spirit," "the divine," "higher power," "energy," or "entity" that will ultimately use that tool to lead them to their desired treasure. Because of that reason, they are directly linked to the metaphysical world, and the use of them certainly warrants a warning.

The Lord rebuked Israel for using such things.

My people ask counsel from their wooden idols, and their staff informs them. For the spirit of harlotry has caused them to stray, and they have played the harlot against their God. (Hosea 4:12 NKJV)

I can already hear how we might try to justify this. "Why

would God be upset by people using a stick or rod to find water? What if they were just thirsty? Wouldn't He want them to drink?" Of course, He wants us to have water when we are thirsty! But first, He is a jealous God. He wants us to go to Him for direction. And I say, why not go to the Creator of the Heavens and earth for direction to what He created? Why do we, as humanity, continue to put our trust in things lesser than God? Does His word not tell us that He is able to supply our every need? We have seen Him supply water in a miraculous way for the nation of Israel when they were in the wilderness.

And the people thirsted there for water, and the people complained against Moses, and said, "Why is it you have brought us up out of Egypt, to kill us and our children and our livestock with thirst?" So, Moses cried out to the LORD, saying, "what shall I do with this people? They are almost ready to stone me!" And the LORD said to Moses, "Go on before the people, and take with you some of the elders of Israel. Also take in your hand your rod with which you struck the river and go. Behold, I will stand before you there on the rock in Horeb; and you shall strike the rock, and water will come out of it, that the people may drink." And Moses did so in the sight of the elders of Israel. (Exodus 17: 3-6 NKJV)

Second, God's word specifically warns us against seeking after direction from any other supernatural means than Him. The bottom line here is that the use of divining or dowsing rods is a form of divination and a practice contrary to God's word.

*You shall not eat anything with the blood, **nor shall you practice divination** or soothsaying.*
(Leviticus 19: 26 NJKV)

Not only is the use of these rods an abomination in God's sight, but it is dangerous! Let's look at it this way. Simply stated, anytime you tap into something where energies or entities can use an inanimate object to communicate, heal, or perform miracles, you are opening a spiritual door to the demonic realm. The repercussions of this are never good! Ouija Boards certainly fall into this category.

Ouija Boards are a little off topic here but certainly need to be mentioned and warned against. If you are not familiar with this, it is a board with the letters of the alphabet, a "Yes" and a "No" printed on it. The premise behind it is that you can ask a question, place your hands on something that will be moved around the board to the various letters spelling out an answer or the "Yes" or "No" words in response to what has been asked. Think about that! Is the board (an inanimate object) actually responding? No, there is a spirit behind it! This is often sold as a children's game. While played in complete innocence or ignorance, there is a spiritual door being opened and an invitation to demons to have an impact on or within the child, even the entire home. If we in fact buy into one of these lies: - "It's just a game," or "I'm not deliberately trying to connect with demons," or "I'm a Christian, so I'm protected," all you are doing is just that. Buying into a lie. A Ouija Board's sole purpose is to connect you with demons. No ifs, ands, or buts about it. Unfortunately, denying you are doing it while you are doing it is certainly no line of defense against what you are inviting into your lives.

Listen, God hasn't given us His word to restrict us or to condemn us! He has given it to us to protect us and to give us liberty! There are two spiritual forces always fighting for victory over our souls, God's and Satan's. The Lord truly desires to protect us from plans or weapons the devil has designed against us. The devil is the master of lies. He will never lead you in truth or to ultimate victory.

For the idols speak delusion; the diviners envision lies, And tell false dreams; They comfort in vain.   Therefore, the people wend their way like sheep; They are in trouble because there is no shepherd. (Zechariah 10: 2 NKJV)

Jesus is the Shepherd who can lead all His sheep safely, and His ways are victorious...every time! The question is, will you follow Him?

CHAPTER 10
Reiki Healing

~ What the enemy wanted me to think ~

I was once invited to attend a Yoga session that was being held in a community indoor pool. The teacher was young, beautiful, and full of grace. She stood up on the poolside so we could all see her from the water and moved effortlessly through the exercises she was teaching. Throughout my journey, it always seemed that I had an instant connection with every new "teacher" and developed a more intimate relationship with them immediately following the first class or workshop. This scenario was no different.

After our session ended, the instructor called me over. She stated that there was an energy about me that she saw and liked, and that she would like to keep in touch and become friends. I, of course, took that as a huge compliment and excitedly exchanged numbers with her. We will call her Ishway. (I made that name up, but it is similar to something that would remind me of hers.) She was, of course, called by another name. It had been assigned to her by a guru, it was not an English name, and it had some deep meaning. It was in one of our future meetings that she introduced me to Reiki.

It was a Saturday morning, I was staring out my front door window, waiting for Ishway to arrive. As she pulled into the driveway, I was getting ready to open the front door but then decided to wait until she got out of the car and made her way up the stairs before doing so. I didn't want to seem overly excited. As I watched out the window, she sat in her car for quite a while. I thought that maybe she was praying. I was thinking, "That's so sweet! She's praying for our session today." I remember trusting her even more after seeing that. After all, I prayed before every session, regardless of what type of session it was. I prayed for protection. I prayed that I would be used greatly to accomplish the purpose that was set before me that day. When Ishway made her way into the house, I asked her if in fact she was praying. She said "Yes." And I was comforted to hear that her prayer was like the one I always prayed. It appeared that we were on the same page.

We made our way down to my basement, where all my psychic readings and energy/crystal healings took place. She gave me a folder with information pertaining to Reiki as she explained the origin of it. (Whether or not this is all factual, this is what was explained to me.) She described how a man had been traveling while on a several-week fast in search of spiritual answers and enlightenment. While sitting, he saw a bright white light and symbols within that light drawing closer and closer to him. These symbols entered his body, bringing with them the power to heal energy blockages, sickness, and disease. This was perceived as a gift from God. He descended from the mountains in which he had been traveling and made his way to a house where he sat and ate an entire meal. This was a supposed confirmation that what he had received was from God. I asked, "Why is that?" Ishway exclaimed "Because you can't eat an entire meal immediately following a fast! You'd get sick!" Having never fasted before, this was certainly news to me. And in my usual gullible fashion, pretty much open to any and everything, I was intrigued and wanted to receive this gift for myself!

This was a special day. Ishway had instructed me to cleanse myself for three days in preparation for what was about to happen. I spent time in meditation, tried to eat healthy, and was as open to all positive energies as possible. You see, I was not only going to experience a Reiki session, but I was also going to receive my first Attunement! A session would mean that someone who was imparted with the Reiki energy would hold their hands above me as I was lying or sitting down. They would move their hands slowly over different areas over my body again, sometimes hovering over me, sometimes lightly placing their hands on me. The Reiki energy or power would heal the energy that was within me. It would release any blockages that would ultimately result in oppressiveness or illness. A Reiki Attunement meant that the power of Reiki was going to be transferred or imparted to me from Ishway, who was a Reiki Master. That from this day forward, I, too, would be able to use this magical power to deliver spiritual, emotional, and physical healing. She went on to describe the symbols of Reiki. Showing me what they looked like and informing me of the purpose of each. They each held specific powers. There were five of them. I do not want to get into the details of them. It's been many years since I've been involved with this and have already had to uncomfortably research some of the specifics, I'm sharing here to refresh my memory. Why uncomfortably? I don't enjoy spending my time researching things of the metaphysical world! In doing so, I have opened up floodgates of memories and experiences that I would have preferred to remain forgotten, but I know it is important for the sake of this book and getting knowledge into the hands of God's people.

She also explained that within each of us, there are seven main energy sources which are called Chakras. They are in specific areas of the body and are responsible for:

1. Your foundation
    a. Being grounded
    b. Your sense of security & stability
2. Your sexuality or creativity
    a. Your emotional connectivity to self & others
3. Your confidence or self esteem
4. Your love or compassion
5. Your communication

6. Your intuition/imagination
7. Your spirituality

The basic principle of Reiki is energy healing similar to that discussed in Chapter 6, however; you are dealing with specific symbols and the "universal Reiki source." While there is a limit to the symbols, I believe there is no limit to the spirits that will avail themselves to be part of this method of healing.

There are a total of three levels of Reiki. Reaching the third, would mean you are a Reiki Master. I was one of those. At level 1 you go through the "attunement" process three times. Each time you are imparted with a different symbol. Levels 2 and 3 are similar in process, but involve different symbols, each designed to open your energetic pathways.

A Reiki Master uses the Reiki energy in both sessions and attunements. The difference is, in an individual session, the energy used is solely for the individual receiving it. The attunement imparts the Reiki energy in such a way that it can now be shared and utilized by that person to bring healing to others. Either way, the Reiki energy enters the body of the recipient. They say that once you have been attuned (imparted) with the Reiki energy, it (or the spirit carrying it), will flow through you for the rest of your life!

Now, I am not sure if the Reiki energy (or associated spirits, sometimes called Reiki guides,) that was imparted to me was stronger than that of others in my metaphysical world family, but the impact or results of my sessions were noticeably different. Perhaps it is because I had now unified the power of these spirits with the powers of the abundance of spirits already using my body as a vessel. This first became apparent to me when I attended a group Reiki session. It was held in someone's spa. Crystal Jesse and I attended this together. We walked in to find the room cleared of furniture making way for a row of massage tables. There were five or so people assigned to each table. We were to take turns laying on the table while the others surrounded us performing Reiki.

Jesse and I were at the same table.

Someone volunteered to lay down first at our table. I took the head position of the table and placed my hands on the crown of her head. As soon as I did that, her body started moving with the energy that was flowing through her. Nobody else in the room was experiencing this, and everyone started looking at us. Crystal Jesse and I thought this was pretty cool! As we rotated through the room, and from table to table, I would see the same results take place for whomever I would place my hands over. It wasn't painful by any means; you could just see the power of the Reiki energy as it made its way through the person's body. With each new person experiencing this, Jesse and I became more and more excited. We were thinking, "Now, that's power!" The rest of the people in the room? Not so much. The owner of the shop later contacted Jesse and told him that they really wanted to maintain the "typical atmosphere" associated with this type of healing. Calm, peaceful, quiet, and soothing. They asked that if we were going to continue in "whatever" we were doing, they would prefer us not to attend future gatherings there. Hmmm.... Really? We were all doing the same exact thing! Could I help it if the results of my healings were more evident? More powerful? (See the spirit of pride creeping in here?) Jesse and I worked together for a few Reiki sessions in private. He then went back to one of those gatherings by himself to find that now everyone he worked with was responding the same exact way! I was thinking "Yay Crystal Jesse! You show them!"

Eventually, as a Reiki Master, I began holding Reiki classes in my home. I was attuning (imparting) people with the Reiki energy. Many individuals studying under me had profound experiences with their bodies involuntarily moving with the energy. Legs would sway side to side if they were laying down, torsos would move up and down, or arms would slowly move in flowy movements, etc. All of this seemed wondrous in our sight, and soon the people who wanted to study under me started to increase rapidly.

Not only were signs of this Reiki method of healing being revealed in involuntary body movements, but there were actual "healings" taking place! And in my opinion, they were most definitely miraculous! As I became more in tune with the "energy" and "spirit" world, the things I was seeing also became more profound! People who would come to me for Reiki healings would lie down on a table. I would start at one end of their body, methodically working my way over their bodies always keeping my hands a few inches above them to "tune into" their body, and "feel for" any energy blockages. Much like what I experienced in Chapter 6, when I was discussing energy healings, my hands would become warm, or I would see a dark spot within the individual. This usually represented an illness or blockage in their body's energy. Sometimes I would see a specific Chakra, usually identified by a specific color, look murky or clouded. That would signify that the specific Chakra needed cleansing. Oddly enough, if I would share what I was seeing within the Chakras, the symptoms the person was suffering from were in alignment with the purpose of that Chakra listed above.

Once I identified an area within the body that required healing, I would gently place my hands on that area and allow the Reiki energy to flow through me into the individual so that healing could take place. In several instances, once I identified the source of the problem, I would (with my intentions) pull that darkness/sickness/disease out of the body. As I would pull (sometimes it would take a lot of physical strength) in an upward motion, the skin on the individual would rise also. I would keep pulling, until it was released, the skin would relax, and I would throw whatever it was into the "protective" white light that I had learned to always surround myself with. I trusted that the spirits in the white light were taking that ailment far away from us. Are you thinking this is farfetched and impossible? So would have I if I had not experienced this for myself. And, if the individual time after time had not gotten up from the table symptom free! People who were not able to stand up straight, stood up, pain free! People who suffered with all kinds of emotional bondage, immediately, seemingly set free! All kinds of sickness and illness...suddenly gone!

Oh, my goodness! Just now I was prompted to open my desk drawer and open a folder that I had no idea was even in there! There are signed testimonies of this attunement process that took place June 4, 2005! Apparently, I had people sign "Experiential Recording Forms" which would allow me to share their experiences of the Reiki sessions or attunements with others. I briefly looked over them to refresh my memory for the purpose of sharing with you what took place. After a quick overview of these forms, I have put together a conglomeration of some of their statements testifying to what they experienced:

One said she had felt a calmness, a stillness, a peace as we began. Some saw different colored lights at different times in the attunement process. One said she could hear the crystals in the room. People could feel the vibrations coming from my hands, that they were gentle and calming. One said she had felt a release of negativity. Others could feel or see a stream of white light traveling through their body. Another stated that it felt pure, another that it was a wonderful experience, and that she was "happy to be me again."

There were pages upon pages, but you get the idea. All this to show you that at that time, in our sight, this was all beautiful, peaceful and done out of a love for and a desire to help people. We all thought I was sharing a gift from God Himself, and it certainly seemed that it was received as such.

~ What God wants you to know ~

There is much to be concerned about when participating in Reiki, at any level. First, it was founded by a Buddhist priest/monk, who saw ancient Sanskrit symbols. It has been said that it was these symbols that helped him develop the system of healing called Reiki. Think about that! A symbol itself has no power! But a spirit attached to it does!

I find it utterly amazing how often I hear of Christians partaking in Reiki. While it is often acknowledged as a "spiritual awakening," my question is, to what spirit? A quick Google search for the origin of Reiki should definitely start sounding some alarms! I did one, and the following Wikipedia definition is what came up: "Reiki is a Japanese form of alternative medicine called energy healing. Reiki practitioners use a technique called palm healing or hands-on-healing through which a "universal energy" is said to be transferred through the palms of the practitioner to the patient in order to encourage emotional or physical healing."

I think the Church has become so numb, so lackadaisical regarding protecting itself against spiritual warfare! So willing to accept anything thrown out there that supposedly would benefit us in some way. But the enemy of our souls, has certainly not slacked off in any way, shape, or form!

Be sober, be vigilant; because your adversary the devil, as a roaring lion, walketh about, seeking whom he may devour; Whom resist steadfast in the faith, knowing that the same afflictions are accomplished in your brethren that are in the world. (1Pet 5:8-9)

The devil is walking around looking for those who are *not* steadfast in the faith! How do we remain steadfast? Stay in His word! Stay in His presence! Anything, and I mean ANYTHING, that has a spiritual connotation or aspect to it, do your due diligence to research it, and protect yourself from the very weapons that might just be being formed against you!

The Church has let its guard down, and in many instances let the thief come in while we were unaware. Unaware or not, if you let him in, open the door for him, you have basically given him authority that the Lord never intended for him to have over you. Let's get to the heart of the matter. What actually occurs in Reiki is that someone is transferring the "Reiki spirit" from one person to another. It is a spirit, guys! And it is demonic. Of course, it doesn't feel or appear demonic or scary; how in the world would the devil be successful in gaining access to so many people if he was to show his true colors? These spirits, even as it is directly taught within Reiki, will in fact stay within a person...forever. The only way to get them out is if they are cast out by the power that supersedes every power, every principality... that is Jesus!

Why would those illnesses, symptoms, etc., seemingly disappear after a Reiki session? For the same reasons I discussed in Chapter 7: Spirits of fear, anxiety, depression, even spirits of infirmity (sickness) would "play dead" or pretend to be dormant. Again, if you no longer feel the effects of them, you think "it's" gone and are no longer looking for ways to be healed or delivered from it.

With Reiki, whether it is recognized or not, we are trying to tap into a power and allow that power to manifest itself through us. The greater the power, the more advanced we are! There is often a spirit of pride that is associated with this. It is hard not to let it take hold. Especially if you don't know and wish to glorify our Lord, Jesus! After all, you are seeing what appears to be all kinds of miracles. People involved with it generally don't reject the glory, and pass it along to Jesus (thank God, because it is none of His). However, the "power" that comes with it can easily boost one's ego. Not only are you now dancing in the demonic world, but you are now exalting yourself to a prideful place. And boy! Did Jesus have to bring me down a few... well...a LOT of pegs!

But he that is greatest among you shall be your servant. And whosoever shall exalt himself shall be abased; and he that shall humble himself shall be exalted. (Matthew 23:11-12)

If we exalt ourselves...we will be brought low. I did, I was. And how extremely thankful I am for the correction of the Lord!

Another side note or nugget of information I would like to share with you pertains to acupuncture. It also works on the premise of healing "Qi" or "energy" blockages within the body. I have seen it stated that Qi consists of equal and opposite qualities known as yin and yang. It is believed by acupuncturists that when there is an imbalance or disturbance between them, it will result in illness. Acupuncture is a technique that is said to restore the balance between these two components by inserting needles into the "channels of energy." While researching this topic, I often saw a reference made to not only physical or emotional healing, but "spiritual" healing as well. Anything that deals with "energy healing" results in red flags, bells, and whistles for me! You will finally see why coming up in the next chapter.

Lastly, I would like to touch on what are labeled as "chakras." The notion that there are different areas within our body that are responsible for different attributes of who we are now seems to me as preposterous! The word of God says we are fearfully and wonderfully made. (Psalm 139:14) We are created with a nervous system that consists of a brain, spinal cord, and nerves that function every organ, cell and tissue within our body. It sounds to me like the enemy of our soul wants us to attribute a special function, separate and different from how the Lord has created us, to very specific areas within the body. He has labeled them as chakras. He has also assigned the colors of the rainbow to them.

Hmmm. Colors of the rainbow, again? The rainbow was a sign of the Lord's covenant with mankind, and every living creature, that he would never again destroy the earth and all that is therein by the waters of a flood. You can read about that in the book of Genesis, Chapter 9. Today, the rainbow is being used time and time again to represent so many things other than this.

Getting back to the chakras. While people may not necessarily think that there are separate or independent areas or entities within each of us orchestrating different areas of our existence, as an outsider (now) looking in, that's what it looks like to me. And truth be told, when you partake in Reiki in an attempt to clear or awaken one of those chakras...there now is.

CHAPTER 11
Mercy said "No"

~ What the enemy wanted me to think ~

All I have shared with you up to this point, has been laying the foundation for this chapter! And as if I weren't deep enough already, you're about to see that I had indeed dug myself a little deeper before the Lord Himself reached down to pull me up. We all know that God has perfect timing, right? Well, right before I was "going down for the count," He threw me a line!

Remember my dear friend, Dot? The one who had helped me grow my psychic business? The one who could hear the sound of the divining rods? Well, the Lord drew her into His church. She, in turn, drew me. One day she gave me a call and said: "Crystal, if you want to feel the presence of God, you've got to come check out this church I found!"

IF I wanted to feel the presence of God? Of course, I did! I thought everything I was doing was of God! For God! On 2/20/05, I went. From the moment service started, I wept in His presence. I asked the person standing next to me "What is this I'm feeling?" They told me it was the Holy Spirit. I had never felt that before! I remember the Pastor asking, "Who here thinks they are going to Heaven?" Yup, in an instance, my hand was waving high in the air! After all, I was a "good girl." I wasn't mean. I didn't do anything to intentionally hurt people; but on the contrary, I tried to help people. And, "God Himself" had given me some incredible gifts! I was seeing miracles all the time! So, yes, I was sure I was going to Heaven.

Immediately following that service, someone took the time

to open her Bible, and show me that according to John, Chapter 3, I needed to be born again in order to make it into, or even see the Kingdom of Heaven. I think you know me enough by now to surmise that yes, once again, I dove in! But this time, it was the Spirit of the Lord and His word that drew me! After a Bible study on the topic, and the word of God gripping my heart, I was baptized the following week on 2/27/05 in the name of Jesus Christ for the remission of my sins! I continued to go to church for the next several weeks, almost instantly falling in love with the people there.

Here is a kicker...I was baptized in His Holy name but still extremely involved with every aspect of the metaphysical world that I have described to you. (I didn't know any better yet.) There were still numerous people who were lost and hurting that I desired to help and would use any or all of the things that I had learned in the metaphysical world to try to ease pain and bring them comfort. One of these individuals was my cousin, (we will call him) Dean. Dean and I were extremely close, more like brother and sister. He had battled with alcoholism for much of his life. The last phone conversation we had; I could literally hear the torment in his voice. He would switch instantaneously from crying out for help to the most eerie, creepy laugh I had ever heard. The battle was real.

It was on the evening of 3/9/05, 12 days after I was baptized. I was holding one of my psychic/channeling parties in the basement. After everyone had gone home, Chris asked me if any new spirits came through during my session. Intrigued, I answered "Yes, there was!" There was actually a male spirit who spoke through me with such power that it made my throat uncomfortable. Almost like he was too big to fit or speak through me. He called himself Allonzo. I was wondering how Chris knew that, or what prompted him to ask. He was expecting a different answer...he said he was wondering if Dean came through. I said "No, why would you ask that?" His response devastated me. Dean had committed suicide earlier that evening. He shot himself in the head while he was at a friend's home. I fell to my knees as grief gripped my heart.

The man who had owned the home that this happened in was like a father to Dean. He, too, was devastated. A couple of weeks after the incident, Chris, my daughters, and I took a ride to go visit that man. I also was on a mission to "clear the negative energy" of the home left behind because of Dean's actions. I went equipped with my crystals, candles, etc., to do the job. After a visit with Dean's friend, he walked us down his driveway to the apartment where it took place. I walked down the stairs, and into the bedroom on the right, instantly feeling a heaviness in the air. I closed the door, leaving Chris and the girls on the other side of it. I set my crystals around the room and started saying my usual incantations. I called on powers and principalities, gods, goddesses, the universe, etc., everything I could think of, to protect myself from whatever horrific thing that had caused Dean to do this unspeakable act, while I tried to cleanse the atmosphere of the negativity. In one instant, all the darkness, negativity, and demonic spirits that had possessed Dean, entered me. I felt crushed. I felt small. I felt defeated, heavy, insignificant, dirty, lost. Like the weight of the world was physically placed on me…in me. I knew something was incredibly wrong, I just didn't know what that was!

Filled with fear, I opened the door to where Chris and the girls were sitting on the steps waiting for me. Chris took one look at me and said, "What's wrong?" Through tears, I told him that I didn't know exactly, but that something extremely bad had happened. After a few minutes in Chris' arms, I calmed down. I gathered my crystals, and we left.

Think about what had just happened. I was already possessed, but now…even more so. The spirit of alcoholism, spirit of addiction, **and** the spirit of suicide (and whatever else was in Dean) was now in me. The next three months were unbearable as I was tormented to the brink of what I could withstand. I had stopped going to that church, although some of the people continued to call. They would ask me if they could pray with me. I would reply "Sure." I never prayed with them, just listened. I had not ever heard anyone pray the way they did. I was raised Catholic. I could say an "Our Father" or a "Hail Mary," but these people were talking *with* God, and on His behalf with such power, anointing, and faith! They would finish, I'd follow their lead, say "Amen," and hang up the phone. The pain was still there.

I would get up each morning and chug a glass of vodka, trying to drown out or stop the torment I was going through. There was a persistent ugliness, uneasiness that was relentlessly swirling around inside me. I would scream endlessly with all my might into pillows, trying to get out of me these horrifying things and emotions that seemed to be trapped inside. I remember wanting to peel the skin off my body to get "out of it." And yup, all the while still practicing every single aspect of the metaphysical world. People were still coming to my home in pain, leaving pain-free. Still holding workshops to teach others what I had been taught. Remember, the last Reiki attunement session I held in my home was on 6/4/05? (over 3 months after I had been baptized). I did not yet understand that all the years of practicing readings, healings, channelings were in fact what had led up to my current state of torment, until one day the Lord opened my eyes. He showed me whom I had been serving all those years and to whom I had allowed access into my physical body.

One evening as I sat on the end of my bed about ready to start a gazing session for myself, I stared at the mirror in absolute horror as my reflection slowly started to transform into something that surpasses even the scariest movie image that I had ever seen…because it was real, and there was no way to "change the channel."

As my image slowly disappeared, a large, dark, hooded figure took its place. It was much, much bigger than I was and literally towered over where I was sitting. More so, it completely took the place of me. The space where my eyes should have been, sank in, and turned fiery red in color. The only way I can describe what I was feeling at that moment was blood-curdling fear and an instant awakening to the fact that I was consumed by pure evil!

I ran from my bedroom and fell to the floor sobbing. The thing is, I knew I could not share what had transpired with just anyone...not even my husband. I thought for sure people would think that I was experiencing some sort of melt-down, or psychotic episode. I kept this to myself for days. Unfortunately, as I have expressed in previous chapters, if you knew you were possessed by a demonic entity, you'd want it out! Of course, I wanted it out! But the cold, hard truth is, once a demon has been exposed, it doesn't leave just because you want or ask it to, and it will do anything in its power to end you. As I have also previously said, if you breathe your last while you are possessed...you are owned by Satan, and it is his kingdom for which you are heading.

I could not comprehend how this had happened! I literally prayed before every session! I protected myself with that white light! I called upon gods, goddesses, the angelic realm, the universe! Everything good! How could something so evil have penetrated that line of protection? If I was not working (teaching, or giving a psychic reading, doing a healing or Reiki session, etc.), I was crying! Sobbing! The demons within me were wreaking havoc in my mind, feeding me unhealthy thoughts about my marriage and my family. They caused me to feel as if I had completely lost control over my emotions. Physically, I felt sick, fatigued, and defeated. Chris was extremely worried with the amount of alcohol I was consuming, but it was the only way I could get even a slight reprieve from what was happening. The alcohol somehow drowned out a little of the darkness. (This was the spirit of addiction/alcoholism.) I didn't want to die and leave my family, but I was beginning to think I should. (This was the spirit of suicide.) There was more, I just can't put it into words. Suffice it to say, I was being tormented for sure.

Right around that time, to my amazement, Jack (the gentleman who trained us on the divining rods), showed up at one of our Wednesday evening meditation group gatherings at Tracy's (yup, I was still attending those) and he was talking with us about demonic possession! How as a "seer" he could actually "see" them. Not only that, but he could cast them out! My heart almost leapt out of my chest with excitement! And to add to my comfort, apparently, I was not the only one in the room dealing with this! There were even workshops being developed and given to teach on how to cast out demons! I approached Jack after the session and made arrangements to meet with him in his office at the campus where he taught. All I kept telling myself was "hold on Crystal, help is on the way!"

I arrived at his office half excited that I just might be set free of this awful thing, half filled with fear, that I just might not be. We talked for a while. He then asked me to sit back and relax as he entered what he called a hypnotic state. He told me that he was going to enter the spirit realm and get rid of the things that had entered me. As he began, I closed my eyes. Something was happening, and it didn't feel good! I did leave his office that day knowing that this was not a done deal. There was still something there. He agreed to come to my house where we could spend more time together and do what was necessary to cast these things out.

During this time, God had opened my eyes to various people in the metaphysical world who were also possessed. Can you imagine? I was living amidst a horror movie! People were coming into my home for healings. I could see darkness in them. Demonic darkness. I would use all the arsenal within my grasp to cast them out...people would experience what they "thought" was deliverance.

Finally, the day arrived when Jack was to come to my home! As soon as he got there, I quickly ushered him downstairs to my basement eager to begin. We talked for a while, then he instructed me to sit quietly while he re-entered the same hypnotic state that he had previously entered while in his office on campus. As he once again entered the "spirit realm to do battle on my behalf," I could feel things digging into me on the inside. It hurt. It was scary. I didn't feel anything leave and shared that with him when he came out of his "trance."

He then instructed me to stand in one corner of the basement, while he stood several feet away, on the opposite side of the room. With his "intentions" and "instructions," he continued to battle with these demons. He would say, "Ok, that one's gone." When he would state that, I would see a dark cloud-like figure somewhere in the room. "There's one!" I would almost scream, pointing to a specific place within the room. He would battle that one, until I couldn't see it anymore. But it seemed as if each time he would get one to leave, another would manifest somewhere else in the room. "Crystal," he said, "you're bringing them in!" What??? Seriously??? How could I? Why would I? After a long while, we stopped. He tried to assure me they were all gone. On our way out of the room, I looked into a large mirror that we have hanging and thought to myself "you're still there, right?" That same dark figure appeared, my hope sank, fear gripped my stomach, and I followed Jack up the stairs.

Eventually, the Spirit of the Lord drew me, and I remember thinking "I should call the Pastor today." I don't recall walking into the kitchen, or picking up the phone, but there he was on the other end of the line. "Praise the Lord, Sister Crystal!" (I was now his Sister-in-the Lord.) I found myself sharing with him that the reason I was not coming back to church was because I was sure he was going to tell me that what I was doing was not of God. But that I knew what I was seeing, and experiencing was not of myself when I helped people, and that I didn't want to stop using the gifts God had given me. That I was seeing people healed! He told me that

I was at a crossroad. That if I stayed on the path that I was on; I would maybe see hundreds healed. But if I stepped onto the path that the Lord had for me; I would see...and then he said a number that was in my mind, astronomical! I'm thinking "biggest sales pitch ever!" He said I was not coming to church based on a fear. That I should just come this Sunday to see what the Lord had in store. I agreed. Then he told me that he wanted to start a Bible study with me. I told him that I wasn't really into the whole "Bible thing," but that I would see him on Sunday.

On 6/12/05, I got up for church. I was excited! Elated! I didn't really know why, I just was. I did not wake my girls to come with me this time. They had attended with me every other time I had gone. For the 40-minute drive to church, I was dancing in my seat bouncing up and down; looking forward to what was about to happen, again, with no knowledge of what that was.

As soon as service started, I again was swept away by the sweet Spirit of the Lord. I had never felt his presence like I did in this church. After service, the Pastor opened the altar for prayer. Of course, I rushed up there. As he stepped in front of me, he said: "Sister Crystal, you and I both know that you are not here because of the conversation we had earlier this week. You and I both know that you've had a run-in with the devil, himself!" As soon as he said that the atmosphere around me was filled with the "Glory of the Lord." It was a light that I cannot put into words. It was different from the "white light of protection" I had been used to. This was almost tangible and so thick that I could no longer see Pastor standing right in front of me. The next few actions happened simultaneously. There was a kind of hush or gasp that came over the congregation. Some of the elders ushered the small children to the back of the church, and the demons within me completely took over! I remember I was thrown to the floor on my back. It felt like my arms were pinned to the floor, but I could feel my body writhing up and being slammed back down. My tongue was coming out of my mouth to a point, like a snake's tongue, and there were growling or snarls coming out of my mouth.

The Saints of God (people baptized in the name of Jesus and filled with His Spirit) gathered around me and battled for my soul. I mean, truly battled for my soul! All I could see was the Glory of God, and all I could feel was the clawing and digging that was happening within my body as the demons clung on in response to the Saint's cries for mercy and deliverance over me. This was a violent battle, but the Saints never gave up. "Come out in the name of Jesus Christ" they commanded with authority in the Holy Ghost. One by one, demons came out with horrific noises as they went. This went on for quite a while, half an hour? Forty minutes? I had lost the use of my body and my voice. I was being completely controlled by what was within me. I was trapped and tormented, utterly unable to speak or communicate the horrific things that were taking place inside my body. All I could do was to cry to God from within myself, in my thoughts. I cried for mercy! I cried "I'm sorry! I'm so sorry! Don't leave me here! Have mercy on me! I didn't know! I thought it was You! Please! Have mercy on me! Help me...JESUS!!!" Finally, with a blood-curdling scream, and what felt like the tearing of my flesh from the inside out, the last demon came out.

As I laid on the floor covered in sweat, sobbing, petrified by what had just happened, I talked with the Lord. "Jesus, if you allowed me to go through all of this, just so I could help people who, like me, are involved with these demons in ignorance...if you allowed me to go through all this, so you could use me to save them...then I need your Holy Spirit dwelling within me." Guys, I didn't even finish that sentence when all that glory that I had seen started pouring inside of me! It felt like it started in my stomach and kept on pouring in until I was completely filled with His Spirit! It felt like He was coming out of every hair follicle on my arms and head…healing me entirely of all that had just happened from the inside out. As His Spirit rose inside me…as it reached my throat…I started speaking in tongues as His Spirit gave the utterance. I sat there for quite some time, allowing His Spirit to speak through me, never wanting it to stop.

I'm not sure how much time had passed from the beginning to the end of this whole episode, but for me it was forever and an instant all at the same time. (If that makes sense.) Once it was all over, I remember speaking to the Pastor's wife. I was so afraid to leave. So afraid to step outside that building. "What if they come back?" I asked. She assured me that because I was now filled with the Holy Spirit of the Living God, no demonic entity would ever be able to enter me again. It took some convincing, but finally, I stood on her unwavering faith, and headed home.

Dot and her children were there and had planned to follow me back to my house after service. It was my wedding anniversary, and we had invited them over for a barbeque. On the drive home I remember thinking "Did all of that really just happen? Was that even real?" I asked the Lord: "If that was real, and your Spirit truly dwells within me, I want to hear you speak in tongues again through me." And He did! I said, "This is a steering wheel." It came out in tongues! I read a road sign. It came out in tongues! And then…it didn't stop! I tried hard to speak in English, but it was only coming out in tongues. I called Dot, who was in the car right behind me with her kids. Her son answered the phone. I tried to explain that I cannot stop speaking in tongues, but again, it only came out in tongues! To my astonishment he said to his Mom, "It's Crystal. She cannot stop speaking in tongues!" I said, "Wait, you can understand me?" He said "Yes, I can understand you." This was completely blowing my mind! Each word that I said to him, in tongues, he translated to his mom in English. I told him I was going to pull over at the next rest stop, he said okay, and we hung up.

I pulled into a parking spot and flew out of my car to Dot.

She had in the interim called the Pastor's wife to explain what had been going on. She put me on the phone with her. I have to say here that I was not afraid in the least! I was filled with overwhelming joy! Peace! Comfort! The knowledge of what God had just done for me...I could not contain my love and appreciation for Him! And He was still speaking through me! Pastor's wife explained that Jesus was continuing to do something through me. He was finishing what He had begun. She said just to let it happen.

We got back in our cars and headed to my house. Once we arrived there, Dot had to explain to Chris and my girls what had happened and why I was speaking in another language. I spoke in tongues 7½ hours that day as the Lord cleansed my house of the demonic entities, I had brought into it. He had me lay hands on the girls. He gently delivered them from every demonic entity that had attached itself to them as a result of my actions. There was no screeching or wailing, no convulsing. The girls were not possessed but oppressed. Demons had attached themselves to them, but they had not entered into them. The girls had not practiced what I did. They never said the incantations that I did. They did not open themselves up to the demons, they were just innocent bystanders. None-the-less, while demons were not given access to their souls, they were able to oppress them through my actions. They still needed deliverance, and Jesus did the job gently and lovingly. Every demonic thing just quietly left in sheer obedience to the Holy Spirit of the Living God that now dwelt inside of me! He then had me lay hands on my husband. Through tears, I spoke in tongues to my husband. I was so sorry for everything I had brought into our home. I was so sorry for exposing him, and our children to what I now knew was evil. As I rested my hands-on Chris' shoulders, I told him I loved him. I was expecting it to come out in tongues, but it came out in English. The Lord had delivered him as well. For He had told me that I would speak in English once He had finished cleaning up my mess.

That day I vowed to serve the Lord, Jesus Christ. I would go where He needed me to go. I would say what He needed me to say. I would tell His truth to those who were being misled and misguided as I once was. Finally, after more than 15 years, and the writing of these first 11 chapters, I am honored to bring to you the conclusion of what He wants me to share with you in the final chapter of this book.

CHAPTER 12
I Give Unto You Power!

~ What God wants you to know ~

The Almighty God is amazing, isn't He? He was the *only* one big enough, strong enough to pull me from the clutches of Hell. The *only* one who could change my destiny from an eternity of suffering to one of bliss in His glorious presence. He is the Creator of the Heavens and the earth, the very sustainer of life, the One who knows all, sees all, *is* all. He is the one who knows, sees, and understands you! He loves you! He wants to be your foundation because He alone is unshakable, immovable and unstoppable! He wants to go before you to fight your battles because He alone is *always* victorious! He wants to be your rereward, (the rear guard of an army), protecting your back when no one else does or can. He never desires for anyone to go through what I did. That is why He gave us His word to use as a roadmap; that we might stay clear of the devil's traps and pitfalls. He gets His word, His plan of Salvation into the hands of those who are seeking truth. Ignorance doesn't save us...but His grace does!

In ignorance, I served the devil for 13 years. In ignorance, I involved numerous people in things that led them to be spiritually oppressed, even possessed. Not knowing the truth didn't save me from being enslaved by the enemy of my soul, *"but where sin abounded, grace did much more abound."* *(Romans 5:20)* Did Jesus, Himself call down "Crystal! You must be delivered! You must be baptized in My name and filled with My Spirit?" Certainly not! But he used people to share His word, His truth, and to draw me unto Himself! It is amazing to look back and see the pieces of the puzzle!

Dot heard about that small church in Kingston, NY (Abundant Life Tabernacle; stop by if you are in the area). She went, felt the presence of God, and told me about it. I went and also felt the presence of God. This was where I was introduced to the Pastor and his wife, whom I'm sure the Lord has chosen to lead me in His ways. Remember that day, after I had come to the knowledge that I was possessed, and I was drawn to call my Pastor? I believe God was drawing me unto Himself as a direct result from my Pastor and his wife's cries for mercy over me. You see, they had been going to Dot's house for Bible studies. One evening, during one of those, Pastor was led by the Holy Spirit into Dot's room and was prompted to look between the mattress and box spring of her bed where he found one of my flyers. That's when the Lord revealed to him all that I was involved with in the metaphysical world. He shared this with me later. He explained how he had shown the flyer to his wife saying "Well, now we know what we're dealing with." They fasted, they prayed, they cried for mercy, and the Lord drew me.

I thank God that I'm part of a fasting church! They were prepared for my day of deliverance!

> *"Howbeit this kind goeth not out but by prayer and fasting." (Matthew 17:21)*

I would like to address the many questions that might have presented themselves after reading the last chapter.

If God loved me so much, if He knew that I thought I was serving Him, being used by Him, if He knew I was being misled, deceived, why didn't He let me know?
He did. He orchestrated all things and people in my life to ensure that I received the truth. After all, that's all I was ever

in search of.

Why wouldn't He get His word to me sooner? Before I became so involved...so possessed? His word says:

"And we know that all things work together for good to them that love God, to them who are the called according to his purpose." (Romans 8:28)

I believe that while I chose to open certain spiritually demonic doors in ignorance, the Lord knew my heart was after Him. He stood with me. He kept me. He ultimately had the victory over me. That eventually He would take everything that the devil meant for evil, and turn it for good, to save many lives... many souls. That even this book, written to expose the weapons of warfare being formed within the metaphysical world against His church is part of His plan. The Lord knew that all I became familiar with through all those experiences could and would be used for His glory.

If I received Jesus as my Lord and Savior, even getting baptized in His name, how could I still be demonically possessed?

Just believing and receiving Jesus as your Lord and Savior (or saying "the sinner's prayer" for that matter) does *not* save you! I marvel at how many people fight against God's *own* word, His *own* plan of Salvation, that leads to His *own* Kingdom. Jesus Himself said:

...Verily, verily, I say unto thee, except a man be born of water and of the Spirit, he cannot enter into the kingdom of God. (John 3:5)

*Marvel not that I said unto thee, **Ye must be born again**. (John 3:7)*

There are two parts to the Born-again experience. According to Jesus himself, we **MUST** be baptized in water **and** of the Spirit. But before either of those can happen there must be repentance. Repentance means that there is a Godly sorrow.

For godly sorrow worketh repentance to salvation not to be repented of: but the sorrow of the world worketh death. (2 Corinthians 7:10)

We need to acknowledge and confess that we have sinned, not to man, but to God.

If we confess our sins, he is faithful and just to forgive us our sins, and to cleanse us from all unrighteousness. If we say that we have not sinned, we make him a liar, and his word is not in us. (1 John 1: 9-10)

Then, we must turn from our sins.

If my people, which are called by my name, shall humble themselves, and pray, and seek my face, and turn from their wicked ways; then will I hear from heaven, and will forgive their sin, and will heal their land. (2 Chronicles 7:14)

Let's talk about being baptized in water. The word baptism is derived from the Greek word baptizo which means to dip, immerse, submerge or plunge. The recollection of Jesus getting baptized, which He did as an example for us, and "*to fulfil all righteousness*" *(Matthew 3:15) states:*

*"And Jesus, when he was baptized, went up straightway **out of the water**..." (Matthew 3:16)*

Jesus tells his disciples the importance of water baptism:

*"And he said unto them, go ye into all the world and preach the gospel to every creature. **He that believeth and is baptized shall be saved; but he that believeth not shall be damned.** And these signs shall follow them that believe; In my name shall they cast out devils; they shall speak with new tongues; They shall take up serpents; and if they drink any deadly thing, it shall not hurt them; they shall lay hands on the sick, and they shall recover. (Mark 16:15-18)*

When I was baptized in His name, I was not immediately filled with His Holy Spirit. The demons remained. It is important to state here that you cannot receive the Holy Spirit if you are possessed. The demons must be cast out first! Once they are cast out, it doesn't mean you are instantly filled with the Holy Spirit, but you are now in a position to receive it. Much wisdom is needed while operating in the Spirit. An individual needs to understand what is going on before you willy nilly go casting out demons! They need to understand the importance of being filled with the Holy Spirit. If you cast out demons without explaining this, you are just making way for more demons to wreak havoc in their lives.

When the unclean spirit is gone out of a man, he walketh through dry places, seeking rest, and findeth none. Then he saith, I will return into my house from whence I came out; and when he is come, he findeth it empty, swept, and garnished. Then goeth he, and taketh with himself seven other spirits more wicked than himself, and they enter in and dwell there: and the last state of that man is worse than the first. ...
(Matthew 12:43-45)

Why is it so important that we are baptized "in the name of" Jesus Christ?

"Neither is there salvation in any other: for there is none other name under heaven given among men, whereby we must be saved. (Acts 4:12)

The power is *in the name*! You will never find in the Bible anyone even baptized "in the name of the Father, Son, and Holy Ghost." Yes, Jesus instructs His disciples in Matthew *28:19-20:*

*Go ye therefore, and teach all nations, **baptizing them in the name of the Father, and of the Son, and of the Holy Ghost:** Teaching them to observe all things whatsoever I have commanded you: and, lo, I am with you always, even unto the end of the world. Amen. (Matthew 28:19-20)*

But look closely! He said, *"in the **name,**" singular...name.* The name of the Father, Son, and Holy Ghost is Jesus!

And without controversy great is the mystery of godliness: God was manifest in the flesh, justified in the Spirit, seen of angels, preached unto the Gentiles, believed on in the world, received up into glory. (1 Timothy 3:16)

Jesus said his disciples should be *"teaching them to observe* ***all things whatsoever I have commanded you…"***
We see time and time again how the Lord's apostles carried forth that commandment. Whenever they baptized someone, it was **in the name of Jesus Christ!** One example of this is when Peter was speaking with the men of Israel about this marvelous Jesus, he said:

"Therefore, let all the house of Israel know assuredly, that God hath made that same Jesus, whom ye have crucified, both Lord and Christ. Now when they heard this, they were pricked in their heart, and said unto Peter and to the rest of the apostles, Men and brethren, what shall we do? Then Peter said unto them, ***Repent, and be baptized every one of you in the name of Jesus Christ for the remission of sins, and ye shall receive the gift of the Holy Ghost.*** *For the promise is unto you, and to your children, and to all that are afar off, even as many as the Lord our God shall call. And with many other words did he testify and exhort, saying, Save yourselves from this untoward generation. Then they that gladly received his word were baptized: and* ***the same day there were added unto them about three thousand souls.****" (Acts 2:36-41)*

Now let's talk about being baptized of the Spirit. You will know if you are filled with His Spirit, because you will speak in tongues as the Spirit of God gives the utterance. His word or plan of salvation doesn't change. This is still happening today, just as it did on the day of Pentecost!

"And they were all filled with the Holy Ghost, and began to speak with other tongues, as the Spirit gave them utterance."
(Acts 2:4)

Now, I have heard it said, "If God tells me I need to be baptized, and filled with His Spirit, I'll do it!" Honestly, that is probably not going to happen. Even when Jesus, the one who wrote the plan, appeared to Saul, who was converted to Paul (the individual responsible for writing most of the new testament), He didn't tell him His plan of salvation. What He did say was *"...Arise, and go into the city, and it shall be told thee what thou must do." (Acts 9:6)* It was a man named Ananias that was sent to Saul with the message from the Lord. He had told him he would be filled with the Holy Ghost (Acts 9: 17), and we see that immediately after the encounter with Ananias Paul *"arose and was baptized."* We see that he was actually baptized in the name of the Lord in Acts 22:16.

If Paul had to leave the presence of Jesus Christ to go to a city in order to receive His plan of salvation from a man, why is humanity sometimes so stubborn in thinking "If Jesus wants me to do it, He should tell me Himself?" God's plan of salvation is shared by word of mouth. Period. That's why He told his apostles to take His message to all nations, to all the world. That's why He counts on those of us that know it...to share it.

I must give a warning here. The devil has even tried to mimic the in-filling of the Holy Spirit. I have heard people speak in tongues in the metaphysical world, but it was not an utterance given by the Spirit of God! This has been called "Light Language" or "Fairy Language". Discernment is needed here! Try the spirit! If it is not in agreement with *all* of God's word, if it doesn't lead to *all* truths, it is **not** the Spirit of God!

Howbeit when he, the Spirit of truth, is come, he will guide
you into all truth: for he shall not speak of himself; but
whatsoever he shall hear, that shall he speak: and he will
shew you things to come.
(John 16:13)

Remember, the devil has some power, but it will **never** be greater than that of God's! Think about this: When Moses and Aaron stood before Pharaoh in Egypt, Aaron threw down his rod, and it became a serpent. Pharaoh's wise men and sorcerers also threw down their rods, and they too became serpents but then we see God's power superseded! *"...Aaron's rod swallowed up their rods." (Exodus 7:12)*

Is it possible to be baptized in the name of Jesus Christ, and not yet filled with the Holy Ghost?

Absolutely. We see in the Bible that just because you are baptized, it does *not* mean you are filled with His Spirit.

"Now when the apostles which were at Jerusalem heard that
Samaria had received the word of God, they sent unto them
Peter and John: Who, when they were come down, prayed
for them that they might receive the Holy Ghost: (For as yet
he was fallen upon none of them: only they were baptized in
the name of the Lord Jesus.) Then laid they their hands on
them, and they received the Holy Ghost. (Acts 8:14-17)

Can you be filled with the Holy Spirit before getting baptized?

Absolutely.

"While Peter yet spake these words, the Holy Ghost fell on all them which heard the word. And they of the circumcision which believed were astonished, as many as came with Peter, because that on the Gentiles also was poured out the gift of the Holy Ghost. For they heard them speak with tongues and magnify God. Then answered Peter, can any man forbid water, that these should not be baptized, which have received the Holy Ghost as well as we? And he commanded them to be baptized in the name of the Lord..."
(Acts 10:44-48)

If I was baptized as a baby, or I was not submerged in water, or if I was not baptized in the name of Jesus Christ, should I get re-baptized?

Absolutely. It is of utmost necessity that you do! There is *one way* to get to heaven. Think about it. Regardless of what you have been told, not *everything* can be true. There is one truth.

"Enter ye in at the strait gate; for wide is the gate, and broad is the way, that leadeth to destruction, and many there be which go in there at: Because strait is the gate, and narrow is the way, which leadeth unto life, and few there be that find it." *(Matthew 7: 13-14)* There is *"**One** Lord, **one** faith, **one** baptism"* *(Ephesians 4:5)*

There is no record of any baby getting baptized anywhere in the Bible. There first needs to be repentance, a baby can't repent and has no knowledge of sinning against God. People who were baptized by John the Baptist even needed to get re-baptized in the name of the Lord:

"And it came to pass, that, while Apollos was at Corinth,
Paul having passed through the upper coasts came to
Ephesus: and finding certain disciples, He said unto them,
have ye received the Holy Ghost since ye believed? And they
said unto him We have not so much as heard whether there
be any Holy Ghost. And he said unto them, unto what then
were ye baptized? And they said, Unto John's baptism.
Then said Paul, John verily baptized with the baptism of
repentance, saying unto the people, that they should believe
on him which should come after him, that is, on Christ Jesus.
When they heard this, they were baptized in the name of the
Lord Jesus. And when Paul had laid his hands upon them,
the Holy Ghost came on them; and they spake with tongues
and prophesied. (Acts 19:1-6)

So, there it is, a scriptural foundation of the born-again experience. You can see now, that after I had been baptized in water, I hadn't completed the whole process. I had not yet been filled with the Holy Spirit, and I, in fact, was still very much possessed and needed deliverance.

When the Lord had opened my eyes to whom I had been serving, and allowed me to see demonic entities within individuals who were still coming to me for healings, were they really being cast out?

No. Technically, I was still serving the devil in the metaphysical world even after being baptized. One thing I used to do in an attempt to cast out demons or clear negative energies from a home or person that I have not yet previously mentioned was called smudging. This practice entails using dried sage (sometimes coupled with other herbs), that have been rolled into bundles. You are supposed to light one end of it and blow it out. The smoke it produces is supposed to have the power to clear the atmosphere or person. It, of course does not, and is part of witchcraft.

So, at that time, I was not filled with the Lord's Holy Spirit and had no power over the demonic realm, but I was certainly on my way to obtaining it! For this same reason, Jack could not cast out the demons that were within me. Our intentions were good. We simply didn't have the authority over them. Only Jesus does! In our cases, it was like the devil, trying to cast out the devil.

"Then was brought unto him one possessed with a devil, blind, and dumb: and he healed him, insomuch that the blind and dumb both spake and saw. And all the people were amazed, and said, Is not this the son of David? But when the Pharisees heard it, they said, this fellow doth not cast out devils, but by Beelzebub the prince of the devils. And Jesus knew their thoughts, and said unto them, every kingdom divided against itself is brought to desolation; and every city or house divided against itself shall not stand: **And if Satan cast out Satan, he is divided against himself; how shall then his kingdom stand?** *(Matthew 12:22-26) But if I cast out devils by the Spirit of God, then the kingdom of God is come unto you. (Matthew 12:28)*

It was the Spirit of God, Himself, who delivered me. Truly, His Kingdom came nigh unto me! I will be forever grateful, forever indebted to this Jesus who I now serve and for whom I live!

During the weeks following my born-again experience, the Lord, in His usual gentlemanly fashion, slowly showed me things in my home that needed to go. Crystals, statues, incense, books upon books, etc. I was thankful for how He took His time with me. He knows all things! All my husband could see was that week after week, I gradually removed more and more items from my home that I had spent thousands of dollars on over the past several years. For me, it was a no brainer, but for my husband, this was all a little much to swallow. He couldn't understand why I was basically "throwing all that money out the window." I would not sell the items, nor would I give the items away. I destroyed them. I was no longer willing to be the vessel opening spiritual demonic doors for anyone!

Jesus desires that none should perish. While He knew I would have immediately done a clean sweep throughout my home if He had revealed all the things that needed to go, He knew my husband would not, could not yet understand. That's why He took his time with this task. I would also like to comment here, that I am so extremely grateful that my Pastor, and His wife did not try to hurry this process. They allowed the Holy Spirit, that now dwelt within me to reveal things in His time. They knew I was seeking God's truth. We did start a Bible study. They faithfully came to my home week after week for years and expounded on God's word. Their son, and another youth, taught my children and several kids from the neighborhood at the same time. They would answer my questions as they arose. So many questions! I think I initially called my Pastor several times a week looking for explanations and answers. Sometimes, he would straight out give me the answer; sometimes the Lord would have him say "Sister Crystal, that's between you and the Lord." And sometimes, he would just start to gently laugh. I could picture him putting his hand to his forehead, shaking his head back and forth. I learned to recognize this as the Lord telling him to just keep quiet on this topic (for now).

Chris did, however, eventually help me burn all my metaphysical books in our wheelbarrow. Gotta say, it was quite the bonfire, and it felt good to watch them burn! It was as if I were watching the chains that had held me captive for so long literally turning to ash. Slowly but surely, the Lord led me to each and every item that held a spiritual connotation. It felt so liberating...truly I was a captive who had been set free!

What does God want you to know now? That He came, suffered, and died for you! He came so that He could make a way for you to join Him in His Heavenly Kingdom for eternity. He came to give you the keys to it and the power to overcome every power, principality, sickness, weakness, illness and disease you may encounter on your way there!

"And I will give unto thee the keys of the kingdom of heaven: and whatsoever thou shalt bind on earth shall be bound in heaven: and whatsoever thou shalt loose on earth shall be loosed in heaven." (Matthew 16:19)

Since coming to the Lord I have witnessed miracle upon miracle! I have seen Him heal people that were diagnosed with two weeks left to live, on more than one occasion. I have seen Him give someone a new bladder, when the old was stricken with cancer. I have seen Him replace a broken bone, with a whole, strong one. I have seen Him deliver many who were held captive and possessed as I once was. The accounts of miraculous healings offered by this gracious, loving God, are more than I can recall, or have space to record here.

I guess the bottom line is Jesus loves us and wants to bless us. Now, and for eternity. When we give the power and authority that Jesus intended us to have, over to the devil through sin, He is there with enough love, grace, mercy, and power to break every chain, and restore that power back to us! He is there waiting with open arms, waiting on a repentant heart, a surrendered heart. Jesus desires to pick you up, and set you upon His rock. He desires to be your foundation; unshakable and unmovable! He desires to shine through you for all to see!

To use you mightily for His glory, and the furthering of His Kingdom! The question is… will you allow Him to?

If this book has ministered to you in any way, shape, or form, I encourage you to find a church that preaches the truth of God's word. Find a church that isn't afraid to teach on holiness standards, and will lead you according to the Spirit of the Lord. Find a Church that operates in the gifts of the Spirit and can teach you to do the same.

He still has much He wants to share with you.

About the Author

Crystal became completely entrenched in the metaphysical world. While what she was experiencing seemed glorious and miraculous at the time, it was essentially leading her to a place of destruction and devastation. Crystal bravely shares her story of practicing psychic readings, energy healings, divining rods, and so much more for over 13 years and how God miraculously delivered her out of the grip of darkness.

Facebook Page
https://www.facebook.com/groups/standingnfaith

References:

https://www.gotquestions.org/chi-Christian.html
https://www.gotquestions.org/energy-healing-medicine.html
Wikipedia
KJV Bible
www.bibleinfo.com
KJV Dictionary
NKJV